Introduction

Look mom, I'm in sales! I've got a catalog, price list, samples, computer, cell phone, credit card, expense account and…………..

Attitude?

     Sales Training?

          Company Knowledge?

               Definition of the target customer?

These questions may sound too familiar to your current organization or companies you have worked for in the past. Having a desk in the sales room does not make you a sales person, no more than owning a set of tools makes you a mechanic. This scenario is no different than assuming someone is a mature adult because they have reached the age of 21 or someone is a safe driver because they didn't have any tickets for the past 20 years.

It's human nature to get to the conclusion as fast as we can. Too often we get caught up into what's on the surface without digging a little deeper to see the real story. The purpose of this book is to give you the proper tools and techniques to develop and maintain a successful career in sales.

Reading this book will put you on the right path. Practicing the processes will help insure success. However, if you don't put the methodologies in your everyday arsenal of sales techniques, all you'll have is another book on the shelf.

This book will walk you through the steps to becoming a successful sales person. It starts with the logic of why you should choose sales as a career and extends into the basics of attitude, appearance, and motivation. From there, we'll explore the importance of your need for knowledge of your respective industry along with various techniques of prospecting. We'll further explore the information you need to process while you're in front of the buyer. Topics such as buying logic - identifies four basic buying personalities that will help you develop the correct sales approach; interviewing essentials - how do you uncover the right information you'll need to advance the sales process; and the art of persuasion - convincing the buyer that you are the best resource for their organization. There are three chapters dedicated to presentations. A review of all presentation facets from the basic materials you'll need through successful delivery are identified. This is then followed by handling objections – identifying, confirming, and resolving. Closing the sale along with departure and follow up – how do you effectively close the sale and what your next steps should be after the close. Lastly, addressed are selling ethics – how do you function in today's multi-cultural business world.

Having spent the first twelve years on the other side of the desk in purchasing, I am able to share some insights as to how to approach and develop effective and successful relationships. I am sharing what I experienced as both the good and bad sales habits. I was fortunate to have had the luxury of experiencing first-hand what worked and what did not, and built my sales career on the successful behaviors of those reps.

I wish you nothing but success. If there is anything I can do to help, please e-mail me at tomvasko@comcast.net.

Copyright ©by Thomas Vasko

ISBN# 978-1495282072

First Printing – December 2014

Contents

Chapter 1: Why Choose Sales?

Chapter 2: Setting the Stage for Success

Chapter 3: Developing Your Selling Skill Set

Chapter 4: Industry Knowledge

Chapter 5: Prospecting

Chapter 6: Buying Logic

Chapter 7: Essentials for the Interview

Chapter 8: The Art of Persuasion

Chapter 9: The Presentation - Basics

Chapter 10: The Presentation - Complete & Competitive

Chapter 11: The Presentation - Make it Clear

Chapter 12: Handling Objections

Chapter 13: The Close

Chapter 14: Departure & Follow Up

Chapter 15: Selling Ethics

Chapter 16: Conclusion

Chapter 1

Why Choose Sales?

If you want decent earnings, freedom and mobility, to always be challenged, and the opportunity for advancement, the sales profession is definitely the job for you. While that all sounds wonderful, it certainly isn't nirvana.

Let's analyze the category that should be most near and dear to a sales person's heart – compensation. Interesting enough, when I entered the sales arena back in the early 80's, most B2B sales jobs were compensated on a draw versus commission basis. The concept has the company paying you a guaranteed salary. However, in return, your commissions need to cover your salary or the company has the right to deduct any shortages from your commission check. That's the basis for draw versus commission. That might sound scary, but depending on pay cycles and your company's commitment to you, you shouldn't experience a problem. Most companies at that time had new sales rep's salaries guaranteed for their first year, meaning there was no pay back expectation in the first year until you developed your account run.

In the 21st century I'm experiencing more salary and bonus compensation plans in lieu of the draw versus commission. The reason this is becoming fashionable is the fact it works in the company's favor. For budget purposes, companies can control the salaries of their sales force on a "not to exceed" basis. They have the salary defined and the bonus has a maximum payout level. In the draw versus commission scenario, commissions were determined by the amount of sales generated by the sales force. In my humble opinion, I believe draw versus commission is the best plan overall. The more the rep sells, the more they earn. The more the rep sells, the more the company earns. I've heard of and actually worked at companies that cap a sales rep's income. While this gives the impression that the company has the upper hand on sales compensation, what they fail to realize is that they have just de-motivated that rep.

Once the rep attains the compensation level of where the cap is established, there is no incentive to add new business or penetrate existing business. The salary and bonus plan has less immediate incentive associated with it. Although, I have heard of salary and bonus plans that have numerous layers of incentives. The challenge with a plan like that is you need to either have a program that is easily obtainable and understandable for the sales reps to keep track of their progress or hire another body in accounting to measure and produce the information the reps need to know for their achievements versus the plan. However, either plan should still afford you the opportunity to make a nice living.

Another trait of a sales career is the freedom it offers. With the technology that surrounds us today, most sales reps could easily work out of their homes. This scenario is a Godsend and a curse all rolled into one. To work out of your house, you need to be very disciplined. Design your home office as you would have your office at your place of work. Eliminate personal distractions – don't put your golf clubs in the same room or have your personal magazines on top of a television next to your desk. Just because you are working out of your house, don't lose the behaviors that did or could make you successful. If you wake up every day at 6:00 AM, don't sleep in until 9:00 just because you are working from home. Know exactly what you want to accomplish that day and don't accept anything less from yourself.

I liked to prospect for new business from home. By accomplishing this task from home, I didn't need to worry about other sales reps listening to my conversations or looking over my shoulder at prospect lists. Conversely, I needed to focus on the task at hand and stay with it until I achieved my goal of appointments, further follow up activities, or other activities to advance the relationship with the prospect. Early in my career, this was an extreme challenge. Hearing four or five no's had me looking for solace in the local sports section of that day's morning paper. The key for me was to take a deep breath, change my message and tone, and give it another try. It just took one yes to give me the confidence boost I needed to continue on that prospecting journey. Maybe it was luck or just my perception, but it seemed it only took one "yes" to get the ball rolling in the right direction. We'll review prospecting activities later in this book, but I used this topic as one of my primary reasons to work from home.

I have witnessed the freedom sales offers sometimes ruin careers. Sales is not a nine to five job. I'll admit there were days when I worked on my short game and putting on a Friday afternoon. However, Thursday evening was spent compiling responses to bid proposals or other customer follow up. Most successful sales people will tell you they have had more days that went from 6:00 AM to 9:00 PM than 9:00 AM to 5:00 PM.

Closely connected to the freedom a sales career offers is the trait of mobility. With our technologically advanced world around us, we have the ability to work effectively from our offices, homes, cars, or while walking down the sidewalk. We can answer voice mails or e-mails while waiting for our baggage at an airport, participate in a conference call while driving to an account, or top off that presentation slide while having that final cup of coffee in the parking lot. No longer is the sales person anchored to a desk or computer. Mobility and the access to instant information have provided the opportunity to connect with more people and accomplish more activities in less time.

Mobility also offers you the ability to better serve your customers in ways that are more customized to their needs and behaviors. When my company first signed on with a voice mail system back in 1987, I had my biggest customer leave me messages with the final statement always being, "call me to let me know you received this message." That kind of drove me crazy because I always wanted to return his call immediately. At the time cell phones were not cheap nor were there enough cell towers to provide good service. This meant pulling off at the next pay phone to confirm I received his message. As his company did not have voice mail, I would typically talk to the receptionist who would transfer me to his extension and since he usually was not at his desk, I would wind up leaving a message with the receptionist. Today, he would more than likely be able to reach me on my cell phone or worst case, I could send a text that I received his message.

As mentioned in the first statement in this section, the opportunity for advancement is golden for sales people. Depending on your organization and its structure, a good sales rep can be the shining star of the company. The nice feature about sales is that you're measured on your numbers; both sales and profits. If you're a successful sales person, you are in demand. Any company would be wise to make sure their successful reps stay with their organization. Competitors in every industry are always looking for the quickest way to get more sales. That "way" is to hire from their competition. Sales reps hired by competitors provide instant additional sales, an entre or rapport with the new rep's accounts they may have not previously achieved, and on the defensive side – they just took business away from their competitor. I'm not suggesting you should change organizations, just implying that if you are successful you can control your destiny in sales.

Another nice feature of a sales career is that you are always challenged. Sales techniques change right along with technology. If I used my approach from the late eighties and early nineties, I would be a failure today. However, using the fundamentals from that time with today's technology has been successful. Being challenged can take on many forms. Sales challenges come in the way of prospecting for new business, maintaining existing business with technology changes within your own organization, making sure your customer's methods of doing business are met. As your organization adds mobility to their business model, so do your customers. They may be looking for Just In Time (JIT) delivery to reduce their on hand inventory costs, adding RFID to their shipments from your company to keep track of their shipments or products from your organization, constant and consistent business reviews to make sure they are taking advantage of the latest developments in the way of products and services in their respective market place. The underlying challenge in all of this is maintaining the relationship with your customers on all levels of the organization. Sales is not a field with designated boundaries. You're given a sales and profit goal and told to achieve it. The good sales rep builds a plan and executes to the best of their ability. There is a wide range of activities that go into the formula for success.

Other working conditions in a sales career include:

- Travel – Design your territory wisely. Depending on your territory, avoid the star route of travel – first call is in the north section, second call is in the southeast area, third call is in the western section, fourth call is in the eastern area, the fifth call is in the southwest, and the last call is back in the north. There will be days when an opportunity arises that will go against this philosophy, but those days should be kept to a minimum. My territory happens to be North America and there are times I need to call on the entire country within a month. My approach is to divide the country up into four quadrants, review flight schedules and pricing and start racking up those frequent flyer miles.

- Expenses – Know where to spend your money. Look at the opportunity the account represents and know how much you want to invest for the potential reward that may come your way. I've witnessed too many reps who take buyers to lunch or ballgames just because they enjoy spending time with them. There's never any "selling" occurring as to how this event will turn into potential sales.

- Customer Contact – Know what your customer expects in the way of communication. Some don't have a problem with a rep just stopping by, others require appointments. Confirm this with your customer. It may sound simple and basic, but it could be a deal breaker down the road.

- Representation – Always be conscious of your image. The business world has appeared to adopt the "business casual" style of attire. Business casual is too wide open for interpretation. For my first few visits or until I have a complete understanding of the organization, I always wear a business suit with a tie. My philosophy is I can always lose the tie, but I can't grow one. Additional image considerations are:

    o Communication, both written and oral. Be professional in your communication. Too often I would see reps who when they were comfortable with the situation would go from professional to talking like they were watching Monday Night Football in a bar. Taking this approach is a quick way to show the buyer your sales approach is an act and the person you present on a sales call is not truly the person you really are.

    o Another part of your image is your car. I've been with sales reps whose cars look like a museum of fast food packaging. Your car is an extension of you – how you think, your organization skills, and your hygiene. Asking a customer to ride in your car that's filled with empty cups, maps, papers, and half-smoked cigarettes shows a lack of respect for them.

    o Another part of your image is your brief case or computer bag or whatever you carry your sales call related materials in these days. Keep your papers neat and organized and easy to find so you aren't wasting a buyers time while you shuffle papers like a Las Vegas blackjack dealer. Avoid keeping half-eaten candy bars and bags of chips in with your materials. Believe me; I've seen it all in my purchasing days.

Actually had a sales rep open his brief case upside down and dump all of the contents on the floor in my office. That was the first and last time we met.

- Lastly, your image consists of the obvious – nails, hair, shoes, and clothing. This may sound basic, but clothing that's cleaned and pressed, shoes that are shined, hair that's combed, and nails that are clipped and cleaned all enhance your image. Don't try to make a personal statement with the way you dress on a business call.

Chapter 2

Setting the Stage for Success

The manner in which you use your time and time management skills could be the difference between a successful or mediocre sales career. Becoming a success in sales is directly related to setting reasonable goals, developing a plan to achieve those goals, and quickly setting new goals. The key fault to avoid in this equation is complacency. It's very easy to congratulate yourself on a job well done; and you should have an accomplishment and reward system. There's nothing wrong with a nice dinner, a new putter, or theater tickets. However, that reward system should not include extending the deadline to accomplish your next goal.

Setting reasonable goals is all relative to your company's goals and what is expected of you. Typically sales goals are related to sales dollars and/or profitability. With that in mind, you should have a definite target goal to establish by the end of the year so you can hit the ground running *(and know where you are running to)* in January. The best scenario I worked with was having my sales goal for the next calendar year established by the beginning of October. For example, I would have my goal for 2012 in October of 2011. This would allow me to plan my sales activities for prospecting, account penetration, price increases, and promotional activities before January 1st.

When setting those goals keep in mind that you are working with a sliding scale. If your target is an additional $500,000 in sales, landing that business effective July 1st will only result in a $250,000 of sales for that calendar year. Likewise with profitability, if your goal is an additional $500,000 in profitability and you land a $1,000,000 account at a 25% gross profit margin, you have only met half of your goal. You won't be successful unless you plan on it. Remember the old cliché, "fail to plan and you plan to fail." Lottery winners are far and few between. Be thankful for the positive surprise, but be realistic and be committed. Remember, there is such a thing as luck, and most times you create it.

Every successful sales person I have ever met has a tendency to worry. They worry about the competition – do they have better pricing than we do, do they have better technology. They worry about the customer - does the customer want to buy from someone closer to their age, are they just using me to leverage pricing. They worry about their own company. Worrying is basically a wholesome form of fear.

Fear is a good and positive motivator. Ask any competitive athlete. Fear is what makes the diving catch in center field or the end zone. Fear is what gives you that extra stride on the ice or court. It's that fine line between success and failure. Fear itself should be used as a motivating factor that brings out your creative side. I would refer to this trait as creative or manageable fear. Fear of losing a customer should make you creative in your approach to keeping a customer. What can you do that will establish a key difference between you and the competition in the eyes of the customer or prospect? How well do you know the competition's capabilities versus those of your company? How well do you know the competition's sales rep or sales team assigned to this account? Does the competitor have a history of how they've approached similar customers or prospects in the past?

Sales slumps, we all have them. Best of intentions, a flurry of prospecting and sales activity, but the end result is little or no sales. Our internal instincts might lead us down a negative path of questioning our own capabilities. The last quality a sales person who intends to extend their career in sales needs is self-doubt. We all have our rainy Monday mornings, but the key to overcoming them is how we dig out of the mental hole we are experiencing. The best thing to do is step back and evaluate the situation. How did the trend change from being successful to striking out? What did you do different? Have trends or technology changed in your industry or with your customer base? What opportunities might you be missing? Too often, sales people become so engrossed with their current buyer that they lose sight of the world around them. Does your current buyer purchase your products for the entire company or is there part of your line that might be applicable to other parts of the company unrelated to your buyer? This is a good time to re-evaluate your current customers and how they match up with you and your company. This is also a good time to look at other opportunities you are or could be working on. This is where you compile a list of your customers. One by one analyze the products or services you are selling them, what you could be selling them, and what improvements could you make to their purchasing habits. Also review your opportunities with your prospects; where are you at in the sales process with them, what can you do to expedite their decision, what approach haven't you tried that could be effective.

It all goes back to the old question, "Is the glass half-empty or half-full?" In my first year in sales, I had four prospects that were going to make their buying decision and all get back to me in the same week. Surprisingly, all four lived up to their word and got back to me with their decision. That was the good news. The bad news is I lost all four opportunities and received all of that news on the same day. That was one of the darkest days in my sales career. All I remember was coming home, pouring a glass of wine and trying to figure out what I could have done differently to change the outcome. Of course that was after a 45 minute ride home where I questioned what I was doing in sales along with a ton of negative thoughts about what do I do now and where do I go next. My level of determination to succeed is what snapped me out of it. The next day I put those prospects in a follow up file and moved on with other opportunities. At the same time, I never forgot that feeling or those opportunities and made a vow to myself to keep going back when I felt I had something better to offer or maybe deliver the same message in a different format. It would have been very easy for me to blame the four decision makers for what I perceived their lack of decision making ability or my company for their pricing policy. Instead, I just said to myself that I will be doing business with them; it just will be at a later date. To give myself a little confidence boost, the next day I called a few customers about existing projects. The feedback was positive and the attitude adjustment was back on the positive side. My confidence was back and I was ready to get after it again. Self-pity over a lost opportunity can be a career killer. Don't let that happen to you. With the social media sites like LinkedIn that offer many sales support groups, there are always resources to talk with and share war stories or get help with a difficult situation you may be facing in a sales scenario. Be resourceful, it may separate you from the competition.

Now onto a more positive sales trait known as self-confidence. To be self-confident you need to believe in yourself. It's very important to conduct periodic reality checks about yourself. Perform an honest assessment of who you are by reviewing your traits that give you this level of confidence.

- Are you well-liked by your peers?
- Do you know all you need to know about your company and their products to effectively represent them?
- Do you know all you need to know about your customers to provide them the best representation that they deserve?
- Do customers and peers view you as a trusted resource?
- Do you seek out methods to improve your knowledge and sales techniques?
- Are you trustworthy?

Just a few questions that may help define who you are as a salesperson. Being self-confident is a trait that puts customers at ease. Expect to make the sale and you probably will. As I did when I lost four opportunities within a day, I gained my confidence back through small victories. Having lost those four opportunities and jumping right back into a high-risk effort, such as cold calling or taking on a large bid could have been setting myself up for additional failure on a grand scale.

Along with self-confidence, enthusiasm is a great trait to employ in sales. If you show enthusiasm about a product or service, chances are very good your customer will react positively as well. Enthusiasm needs to be sincere. Customers for the most part can tell when it's not genuine. If you come across as self-confident and enthusiastic and are proven to be a fraud, it will take you a long time to rebuild that image and instill confidence in your contacts. The key to exude genuine enthusiasm is to know your product or service, know exactly how it will benefit the customer, and know how you compare in quality and price to any potential competitive products or services. If you do your homework, your self-confidence and enthusiasm will be apparent in front of your customer. This isn't to say the sale is guaranteed, but you'll give the customer more reasons to want to buy from you. The characteristics of self-confidence and enthusiasm tend to play off of each other.

You always want to enter a sales situation with a sense of enthusiasm and confidence. I'm not big on self-motivational speeches and banging my head against the steering wheel to get my juices flowing before a sales call. For me, it never hurt to listen to a good piece of music (Led Zeppelin, Van Halen, or Chicago) or a good comedy CD before going into a sales call. Something about these two genres that just made it easier to smile and be relaxed during the call.

Being in the right frame of mind can make all of the difference in the world on a sales call where you have a finite time frame to effectively convey your message so your audience understands and agrees with you. If allowed, a negative thought or emotion could sidetrack even the best sales person who isn't prepared to absorb it and turn it around to their benefit.

In the early stages of my sales career I had the opportunity to present to a large bank group. I had been waiting for this opportunity for almost a year. The morning of the presentation was a disaster. There was a horrific storm going through Chicago that morning and my car which was fairly new wouldn't start. Nothing I can do about the rain, but I finally did get the car to start. After a fifty foot sprint from the car to the bank with three presentation binders, a brief case, and an umbrella, I achieved my first level of success – I was safely at the bank. Next step - up to the executive vice president's office to set up my presentation for him and his assistant. His secretary was so gracious saying I could take my time to set up and use the restroom to dry off and instructed me to just leave my umbrella in the corner of her work area.

I thanked her for her kindness and foolishly opened the umbrella which sent a spray across her work area, luckily not at her. This is where I thought my luck had reached the end of the line. She just laughed and said it could be worse, not to worry about it. Although I tried not to show it, I was really upset with myself. It was probably her pleasant demeanor that put me at ease.

The presentation went well, much better than I expected. The executive was an old military man, who you could tell by his appearance liked everything in its proper place. Delivering a logically structured presentation to the executive was the best solution for a challenging day. However, after the presentation was over, he thanked me for my time and professional approach to dealing with his organization. I almost started to feel comfortable and then he asked me that question I never heard in all of my sales training, "who is your competition?" Being self-confident and enthusiastic about this opportunity, I replied "you can open the yellow pages and look in the product categories I'm proposing to you. You will see a list of names, but you won't see anybody who offers the products and surrounds them with the services that we provide." He just smiled and said, "Great answer, let's get started." Without confidence and desire and given the situations working against me that morning, I would have cancelled the appointment.

Another topic related to a successful sales career is that of time management. Here is another trait that if left undeveloped, will ruin a sales career. The successful sales person will always have the characteristic of being a self-starter. This is a person who knows what they are going to do, how and when they are going to do it, and then does it. They aren't waiting around for the next set of instructions. They have a plan and they execute that plan.

How do I become a self-starter? Simply stated; set reasonable goals, develop a plan to achieve those goals, execute the plan. It all begins with a plan for success. Once you have your plan defined, you then need to develop strategy for how you are going to make those accomplishments a reality. A self-starter is someone who possesses the internal drive for success and isn't satisfied with the minimum acceptable performance. Their target is always to exceed expectations. Once their strategy is in place, they work at it – win or lose. They continue to work their strategy and adjust as needed.

One question self-starters typically ask of themselves is, "how do I get more out of my day?" Is there an opportunity to better manage your time to accomplish more or achieve more success in a shorter period of time? The easiest way is to always plan your day, week, and month. With all of the electronic calendars and CRM type systems available on the market these days, there is no reason to be fumbling around with notes all over the office with follow up instructions or potential meeting dates. The resources available to keep sales people organized today are phenomenal. You have schedulers, reminders, and task lists which can be synched to your phone or home computer and probably your car sound system. As a result of this available technology, you should have access to your schedule at any given moment. If you have all of your events organized in one place, it will make it that much easier to schedule your next meeting versus the "let me check my calendar and I'll get back to you" which just further delays the opportunity for a meeting and potentially gives the buyer an "out" to avoid scheduling the meeting.

Another way to get more out of your day is to effectively manage your territory. With traffic patterns and the price of gas, managing your territory will not only add more time to your day, but keep a few dollars in your wallet. Whether your territory is North America or the northern part of your town, always try to work in the most time effective driving pattern possible. Using this method may allow you to see an extra customer or two per day or give you time to finish those administrative tasks before sundown instead of working into the evening. There will always be the exception to the rule of a prospect or customer who wants to see you on a Friday afternoon and they are twenty miles from where you want or need to be. At that stage it's time to weigh the benefits versus the risk.

Another characteristic is to organize the materials you carry with you. Whether it's a brief case, shoulder bag, or simply a laptop in a computer bag, consider this an extension of your desk or office. When you open this bag in front of a customer, they don't want to see a stack of papers askew on top of a half-eaten candy bar or sandwich. The customer should see something that resembles an organized thought process. Early in my career, I managed a purchasing department. I witnessed sales reps who couldn't find their car keys at the end of the call because of their lack of organization. However, I did note that the successful reps were always those who were well organized and made a good appearance.

And lastly, allow time in your schedule for those dreaded administrative tasks. Depending on how you interface with your customers and the support staff you have back at the office, you might be surprised at how much time these tasks can use up of your time if left unmanaged.

Start with a positive attitude, good appearance, a set of aggressive and attainable goals, a plan to make those goals reality, and then do it! Don't worry about what you didn't accomplish, plan on how and what you are going to accomplish.

Chapter 3

Developing Your Selling Skill Set

You probably cannot count the number of times you've heard someone say "that person is just a born sales person." This statement implies that there is a gene that every successful sales person possesses that separates them from the non-salesperson. I'm not a scientist or medical expert, but I would be willing to bet the "sales gene" theory is not quite accurate. Typically someone receiving the designation of "born salesperson" has an outgoing personality and may even be persuasive. In reality, there is no such animal as a born salesperson, so let's look at the ways you can develop your selling skill set.

Let's assume that every characteristic from the first two chapters is in place – attitude, organizational skills, appearance, goals, and the plan. Now what do you do? You go on that treasure hunt for customers. This is called prospecting. We'll have an entire chapter dedicated to activities related to prospecting later in the book. For the sake of this chapter, prospecting involves the art of selling the prospective client on the idea that by taking the time to talk or meet with you, they will save time or money, or in some way improve their livelihood.

The first step in developing your selling skill set is that of effective communication. That is how do you convey your message to a prospect or customer so they can understand everything you are saying? The best example of this I ever witnessed occurred in a sales 101 class in college. Our professor walked into the room, introduced himself, walked over to the first desk and dropped his sport jacket on the floor. The professor then asked the student to instruct him of how to put his sport jacket back on. This exercise lasted twenty minutes as a result of the student needing to provide explicit instructions to retrieve the jacket from the floor all the way through buttoning the top button. The key message from this exercise was to never assume the customer completely understands your message. Always confirm with the customer that they comprehend the features and benefits of whatever you are proposing to them. In the case of the above exercise, you could see exactly what was understood by the actions taken by the professor.

Whether or not you realize it, everyone consciously or unconsciously, is a sales person. At some point in our daily lives we try to sell an idea, product, concept, or opinion to someone. The person on the street asking for spare change or displaying the "will work for food" sign is trying to sell us on the idea of supporting them with a donation or a job. This may be an extreme example, but it is still selling. A child in a grocery store throwing a tantrum because his parent would not buy them a toy or candy bar is actually selling – buy me what I want and I won't embarrass you in front of the other customers – win / win. In reality, sales people come in all shapes and sizes.

Early in my career working in the mailroom at Kraft Foods, Dan Walker, the gentleman in charge of sales promotions and in-store activities, approached me with the question of what did I want to do with my life. I was all of eighteen when he asked that question. My answer was most likely somewhat vague, but I am sure that it did not include the word sales. He quizzed me as to what were my thoughts about sales, to which I probably responded with an answer about silver tongued devils wearing loud suits. Over time, Mr. Walker would catch me around the office and have brief conversations with me about sales and why he thought I would be a good fit for that career in the future. His words never left me, and I can count him as one of the major reasons I'm in sales today. I only wish that he were still alive when I finally did land my first sales job.

As my career developed after my tenure Kraft, it took on more of a purchasing flavor. By managing the purchasing process for various organizations, I came in contact with a multitude of sales people. These experiences helped shape the sales person I became or in some cases, did not become. In fact, the best sales people I dealt with were in a minority. The successful reps all possessed the same qualities – returned phone calls and provided information in a timely manner, followed up as necessary, personable, honest and resourceful - even if it meant they didn't secure the order. They made it difficult to not want to buy from them.

On the other hand, I learned a lot of what not to do. To this day, I cannot believe how many sales people had little or no follow up skills. They were so focused on the first order, they never saw the opportunity for the second, third and subsequent orders. The first mistake is to assume you have the business locked up because of your relationship with the previous buyer. Case in point, as a new buyer I was meeting with our printing sales rep who managed all of the internal documents the company used in their daily operations. The gentleman entered my office, introduced himself and said nothing else to me for about ten minutes until the old buyer came to my office to explain the relationship between our two companies. This gave me a prime indication that he had no interest in me, my history, or any thoughts I had on the relationship going forward. After I tried to make small talk about the weather and traffic, there was still no reaction. Incidentally, that was our last meeting. My new printing source met with me the following day. Other traits I found irritating as a buyer were people who just dropped by unannounced, reps who were consistently late, reps who did not listen as to what we did or did not need and presented a product or service that was not applicable to the organization. I always wondered if their companies knew the bad impression these reps were giving potential customers. You can easily lose an opportunity by what you don't do as much as making a mistake on an order or service request.

The most ideal method of developing an effective set of selling skills is for you or your organization to hire a professional sales trainer or internally conduct a professionally designed training course. This should be a course that is general enough to address all of the sales scenarios you may face while targeting specific issues to your product line(s.) My initial sales training consisted of The Professional Selling Skills developed by Xerox Corporation, as well as numerous sales training books. Also included was a three month period of internal training within the various departments around the company. This helped me learn products and services that I should or should not commit to when selling the services of my organization. I'm aware of quite a few companies who discount the importance of a good sales training program. Ultimately, they would pay the price by on-the-mistake training. Incorrect products would be sold for an application or services that did not exist would be promised to a customer.

So what additional traits do you need to have to be successful in sales? You will need to develop traits related to your personality. Those traits are – your drive; characteristics – shaping that first impression; conversational habits – the sound behind the person; and mannerisms – how you do what you do.

Let's review your personality. To be a success in sales, you need a high level of drive and dedication. This is interpreted as not being afraid to work hard and smart. Depending on the product or service you sell, this could require you to work until the wee hours of the morning. You need to be prepared to take on the challenges when new opportunities present themselves. I have never heard a sales rep say that a prospect or customer gave them too much time to prepare for a meeting or a response to a bid. The successful sales person takes every opportunity that arises, immediately analyzes the potential benefits, and determines a plan of action required to accurately prepare a response to the request. Assume you will be working under tight time frames, and any opportunity with a reasonable lead time will seem like a bonus. The key to these situations is working smart. Know the resources available both inside and outside of your organization. Dedication is one of the key personality traits required for success in any field, not only sales. If you are not dedicated to the success of your organization, your customer's satisfaction, and yourself, you will not succeed anywhere.

The second part of your personality required for sales success is intuition and common sense. This isn't only about your intelligence level; it also relates to how well you are able to converse with different people at different levels, which is also important. The ideal sales situation is to develop a relationship at various levels within your accounts. For my key accounts, those who represented 80% of my income, I had developed good relationships with everybody from the receiving department to the president and anyone in between who had contact with me or my company. To establish those relationships, you need to be able to have conversations on various levels. The key here is to know your audience. Be very aware of the industry you are calling on and what hot buttons exist in that field. For example, if you are calling on the banking industry, it would be helpful to know of any pending legislation that could have an effect on how they conduct business in the future. In general, it helps to be well rounded and at least be somewhat familiar with the major events going on in the world. A quick two minute scan of CNN on-line can provide a quick overview of current events. You don't need to know the score of the Kansas City versus Seattle game last night, but it couldn't hurt to know who had a recent major effect in the sporting world. This all comes down to knowing your customer and the contacts within that organization. When having those conversations about someone's favorite topic, be sincere. That one little tidbit of information that you deem insignificant, may be important enough to secure another ally within your customer's organization.

Another key piece to your personality trait is the willingness to be trained. This goes back to dedication and the thirst for knowledge or intelligence as we just discussed in the previous paragraph. Successful reps always live on the cutting edge of new approaches available in the market place. It relates back to ridding yourself of old paradigms. There is a major difference in calling yourself an office products distributor or a distributor of products for the office. The name office products distributor conjures up a picture of pens, paper products, and general supplies used in daily operations in an office. Distributor of products for the office paints a picture of everything contained in an office setting. You're not limited to just the general supplies, but furniture, space planning and design, coffee services, and potentially other services required by various operations within a company. It's getting people to think beyond the thought of what have we done up until now, versus what are we capable of doing.

Recently, I was scheduling a sales meeting and added a sales refresher course to the agenda. I asked our sales reps if there were any particular areas they would like to see addressed as part of the training. Unbelievably, one rep actually responded with, "I used to perform sales training at one of my previous employers. I don't think I need any additional training." I reviewed her resume as I didn't recall having that conversation with her five years ago when she was hired. It turns out she did perform sales training over twenty years ago. During our next conversation I asked her if she thought things have changed over the past twenty years as it relates to sales strategies or just selling in general. I also added the caveat that there was a right and wrong answer to that question. Just so you know she did get it right. If you're still doing things the way you were 2 or 25 years ago, you are definitely heading in the wrong direction. Training, whether remedial or a full blown program, is essential to stay at the top of your sales skill set. The training could relate to product improvements, new product availability, sales skills, or anything related to making you more of an asset to your company and your customers.

An additional trait for success is that of your personal features. Appearance, clothing, and hygiene are the most obvious factors. However, there are also those traits that relate to your physical characteristics such as health, posture, and any disability. Let's start with health. We all come in different shapes and sizes. There isn't any rule of thumb that says anyone thirty pounds overweight or less than 5' 9" tall cannot be successful. The key issue related to health is to present yourself in a professional manner. Don't get on the phone if you're in any stage of laryngitis or whooping cough. Don't go on a sales call if you're battling a fever. You may believe that you're a hero for doing this and you're showing the customer that you'll be there regardless of how you feel. Unfortunately, you are also running the risk of passing your illness on to your client. This is one thing from you they definitely do not want from you. A timely phone call from you to reschedule your appointment is the best approach here. Do your best to maintain good health for more reasons than just being successful in your career.

Also your posture can say a lot about you. Present good posture by standing erect and avoid slumping your shoulders or hunching your back. The bottom line is don't give the appearance of being defeated. Stand erect, look confident and give the client a feeling of reassurance they are working with someone in control. You may have just experienced the toughest day of your career, but don't transfer those feelings to the opportunity in front of you.

As it relates to disabilities, all you can do is your best to avoid making the situation uncomfortable for either party. Everybody deals with this situation in their own way. There are temporary disabilities such as people using crutches or wearing casts to overcome broken bones or torn ligaments. Those situations are usually a discussion piece. I'm speaking from personal experience as I've had a broken knuckle and a torn Achilles. Sales reps using wheel chairs or artificial limbs should just go about their business as they normally would. You want to avoid the disability being the centerpiece of your meeting. However, at the same time, you want to present an image that aside from your physical challenge, you are no different than anyone else. You have the same personality traits, personal characteristics, and sales skills that everyone else possesses. The disability isn't who you are.

Quite some time ago a sales rep made a "goodwill" call on my company to make sure their equipment was functioning as it should. I happened to be passing by the area as he was performing his diagnostics and asked if there was an issue with the communication equipment. He replied there was not a problem and proceeded to introduce himself. As I stuck out my right hand, he responded by sticking out his left hand, which I found odd at first until I noticed he had a prosthetic hook for a right hand. I chose to ignore that fact; we shook hands and had a brief but informative impromptu meeting afterwards. I knew I was the one who felt uncomfortable for about three seconds and he proceeded as though it was just another day in the field. He handled the situation like a professional and the focus quickly became his purpose for the goodwill call, not his disability.

Also important are conversational habits. This area entails the words you use and how you use them. Too often this area receives very little emphasis. The general assumption is that because you are in the sales arena, you know how to speak. And while that's true, there is a difference between having a casual conversation with your friends and a business meeting or presentation with a client. Let's first start with the words you use. With the ability to check virtually any company's website, you have a head start on becoming familiar with your prospect or client's culture. I would strongly suggest visiting the various pages of their website to learn their mission statement, any social or environmental commitments, their product lines, and their customers. Also look for any company *"isms"* – is there verbiage they consistently use in their communications. If you speak their language going in, there is certainly one less hurdle to overcome. You can certainly gain an advantage walking in the door armed with at least some basic knowledge of your prospect or client. Another thought is know your audience and what you are going to say. Don't use verbiage people cannot relate to, nor should you use words of which you don't know the meaning. More than likely, the industry you work in has a language all of its own when referring to systems, equipment, or services. While it's okay to use that jargon at the right time, make sure that you provide a full explanation of the meaning the first time it's used. Don't make assumptions everyone knows what you are talking about. You could be talking yourself right out of an opportunity.

So now that you know what you are going to say, let's review how you are going to relay that message. Enunciation is so important in delivering your message. Ask any speech or theater major and they will tell you that enunciation is a key factor in public speaking. Why go through all of the effort of researching a company, getting those first appointments, compiling a professional presentation and then delivering it sounding like your head is in a bucket? Speak clearly and succinctly so everyone can understand you. Also, keep in mind your sale depends on your customer clearly comprehending your message.

Make sure to project your voice, don't talk to yourself. If you're presenting in an office or conference room, after delivering the general benefits statement, ask if everyone can hear you. That is the time to get confirmation of whether or not everyone can hear you. Unless someone has paid to hear you speak, they are usually not going to indicate they cannot hear you. Why lose the opportunity to deliver your message when you've worked so hard to develop the opportunity? Make sure you're heard! Also, tone placement is vital when emphasizing an important part of your message. Don't read your presentation, that's an insult to the buyer's intelligence. If you're using a printed or a more formal PowerPoint presentation, vocally emphasize the key points and elaborate. Presentations are a guideline for the message you want to leave with your audience. I've sat through flip chart and PowerPoint presentations that made me feel like I was back in third grade. The only thing missing was the wooden pointer. Don't do that. You don't need to emphasize every sixth word like a rap star, but know what is important and what your audience _should_ hear. Practice, practice, practice your presentation ahead of time. Appear comfortable and in control, don't appear like it's the first time you are hearing your message.

Next are vocal mannerisms and we all have them, which come into play in presentations. Having teenagers, I've noticed this trend where they sound like they're asking a question at the end of every statement. I notice if I don't respond with an *okay,* they won't continue on. I've just learned to respond with an *I'm still listening.* However, when presenting, using the upward inflection at the end of a sentence is important when you want to obtain feedback or gain confirmation from your audience. But please don't use that quality after every sentence. You'll give your audience the impression that you are unsure of what to say next or that you need approval on each and every point.

Speaking of being unsure, stammering is a trait you want to eliminate altogether. We've all experienced a moment when you're asked that zinger of a question and you raise your eyes to the sky looking for that magical answer from the sales heaven. The first reaction is to answer the question even though you truly don't have an answer. This usually results in that stammering moment, where the uh's and oh's happen every other word. A polite pause is acceptable, but you don't want to verbally trip over yourself. The best approach is if you don't know the answer, repeat the question to make sure you have the correct question to which you need to obtain a response. Politely say you will contact the correct source for an answer to the question, confirm that your actions are acceptable to the person asking for the information, and move on with your agenda. A sales rep that attempts to make up an answer on the spot runs a very high risk of being exposed as untruthful or a fraud. Remember how hard you worked to get this opportunity. Why lose it because you wanted to appear to have all of the answers?

Finally, let's review manners and mannerisms. This is where a good many sales reps fail to understand that when you are in front of a customer, you are in their house and on stage. Like your mother probably told you since you learned how to walk, *"be on your best behavior."* Be considerate and empathetic. My rule of thumb was to always be ten minutes early for an appointment. If my customer could meet with me, great; if not, I had ten minutes to talk with the receptionist to learn more about the company and gain another internal ally. As a buyer, I always liked when a sales rep was a little early. It added flexibility to my schedule. When initially meeting with buyers, it's always a good idea to know how much time they have allotted for the appointment. Even though you may have stated a timeframe when scheduling the meeting, circumstances may have changed since that time.

Showing consideration of a buyer's time will certainly help strengthen the relationship. Empathy for your buyer and their organization is certainly a key factor in developing a good long-term relationship.

Become familiar with their top priorities for selling to and servicing their account. When you're interviewing your prospect for the first time, develop a list of questions not only pertinent to their business, but also how that individual prefers to operate. Never assume two clients are alike or have the same preferences. Also, during the initial interview as well as all subsequent meetings with anyone, have good listening skills. When you ask a question, wait for the answer. Too often I've witnessed a sales rep ask me a question, then look down to see what the next question is they are going to ask without listening to my response. Good listening skills are essential to a successful sales career and life in general. If you don't possess those skills, make it a point to develop them.

Always speak respectfully of others. Whether it's people in your organization or a competitors, don't trash anybody. If a buyer shares a story about a poorly performing competitor, the best response is to act surprised and thank them for that information. My thoughts were that if a competitor is still in business, there is someone who must like them. Also, if your client is sharing stories about the competition, they may also be sharing stories about you. Don't give them any ammo to use against you.

Although it may be difficult in a high pressure situation, always act natural and appear relaxed. You cannot and should not let the client know you are in an uncomfortable situation. A good example is a time when I changed companies and went to work for a competitor. My former company targeted my key accounts and pursued them relentlessly. Although I converted most of my key and secondary accounts, my largest account informed me they would split the business and see how each of us performed. After the ninety day trial, the buyer informed me he was going to conduct another trial period where each of us would be the sole supplier for ninety days and after that time period he would select one supplier. What made it worse was my competitor would get the first ninety days. At that very moment, I knew I became a salesman. My mind went into panic mode, but my body language didn't show it. I sat back in the chair and confirmed that we were doing everything he required of a supplier. After that, I went through all of the process improvements we made on his behalf from the day we started doing business. At the end of that list, I received confirmation that he agreed with those points. I then closed the deal by asking that my company get the first ninety days of the trial. The reason for wanting the first ninety days was I knew I would develop a strategy to circumvent him trying the competitor. I'm proud to say the goal was accomplished and we were awarded the sole contract on a national basis. In retrospect, had I not challenged the buyer to give my company the first trial slot and shown my inner emotions, the business could have easily gone the other way.

Other mannerisms to keep under control are nervous habits. I've been with reps that drum on the arms of their chairs, crack their knuckles, or click the cap of their pen. While they are nervous mannerisms, they can serve as a point of annoyance to a buyer. A former company I worked for had a few employees in their finance department that had various nervous habits – voice inflections, nervous twitches, always ending the sentence with "hmmm?." I remember coming out of meetings with them and noticing a faster heart rate. While I personally liked these people, sitting in a room with them for hours reviewing budgets was challenging.

These last two habits are fairly easy to control or overcome. The first habit has been outlawed in most buildings, and that habit is smoking. If you do find that oasis where smoking is allowed, I would strongly suggest asking your customer for their permission before lighting up. If I were a smoker, I would avoid this at all cost. Fortunate enough for me, I had the inner strength to overcome this habit over thirty years ago when cigarettes were still under two dollars a pack.

The second habit is using vulgar language. Some people feel the need to use this when they are in a comfortable situation, thinking that they no longer need to work at their image. Once, after interviewing a sales rep seeking employment with our company, he was waiting in my office for one of my sales managers to meet with him for their portion of the interview. I decided to make small talk with him about Sunday's football game. That was probably the best question to ask, because I learned more about his personality traits than I did asking business and sales related questions. The vulgarity came spewing out of this mouth about a call or series of plays. Needless to say, he was not asked back for further interviews.

In summarizing this chapter, make it a focus to be the best individual you can be and present those traits to your clients. Nobody is perfect, but don't sabotage your own sales efforts because of a trait that could be easily corrected. A good sales rep is trained, shaped, and molded; not born.

Chapter 4

Industry Knowledge

How well do you know the capabilities of your organization, of your competitors, history of your industry, new trends in place or in the rumor stage? Without this basic knowledge, you shouldn't even attempt to make a sales call.

With regards to your own organization, can you define your product? Is it the actual product that's in your catalog or website, be it a manufactured item or an intelligence based product such as consulting services or customized software? Is the product the special services offered that make it easier for the customer to work with your organization? Is the product you? Depending on the situation and the company, the answer could be all three. As an example, I sold for a national distributor of products. The actual products were those shown in our catalog. However, we also surrounded those products with service options to make it easier for the customer to order and receive the products, as well as provide reports and invoices to charge back departments if required. To prevent over selling unnecessary services, I had to know the competition and what they were capable of providing so I could effectively sell against them. At the same time, I needed to develop a strong relationship with the prospect or customer to prevent a situation of other competitors trying to take the business from our organization. In this example, the products were the actual items the customer could purchase, the services we provided to satisfy the customer, and the representation I provided that strengthened my company's relationship with the customer. It is absolutely tantamount to know your organization's products and services. The best organizations I ever worked for provided intense training for the first few months of my employment. Without a clear and concise understanding of your company's capabilities, you cannot be very effective on a sales call.

As a new sales rep, you should want to acquire as much knowledge as you possibly can. Talk with other sales reps, read industry journals and blogs, if you're a distributor talk with some of the manufacturer's representatives, or look for a trade association to join. Knowledge is available from many sources, especially via the Internet. Social networking sites such as LinkedIn could be a valuable source for networking within your industry.

As long as we are talking about acquiring knowledge, how much do you know about your competitor? What do they do, how do they do it? What do they do better than or not as good as you or your company and vice versa? What do you know about their sales reps? Are they a diverse group of people, meaning do they have various sales talents that would require you to know exactly who you are selling against? Do they have reps that only sell on price, while others who are very competent and sell the entire package? What do you know about the services they offer? Are their capabilities better, worse, or the same as your organization? How do you sell to your strengths and minimize your weaknesses? How do you create a competitive difference? Just a few things that are important to know before you turn the key in the ignition.

As an example, I was given an account from a sales rep that was retiring. This account company employed over one thousand people. Applying an industry standard, this account had an estimated value of one million dollars annually. At the time I assumed responsibility for this account, my company had annual sales of fifty thousand dollars to this organization. I immediately schedule an appointment with the buyer and compiled a list of questions as to why we were not getting the lion's share of the business. Obviously, I didn't use those exact words, but compiled a list of questions based on our strengths and services offered other accounts of their size and operation. The meeting went surprisingly well. I was able to uncover the competition - both company and sales rep, the services they were providing, services my predecessor would not provide and the logic or lack of to support his actions, as well as the greatest piece of information I could have received – "if you want the majority of our business, here's what you need to do." I had a definite game plan going forward. I already knew my competitor and their strengths and weaknesses. We matched up well against them. I then talked with other reps at my company about the sales rep from the competitor and determined he was a rep who quoted prices and nothing more. He did not sell services, nor did he function in a consultative manner. The agenda for the follow up meeting was set. It consisted of all the points I needed to meet in order to convert this account. Within two weeks of my first sales call to this organization, I was on track to realize annual sales of $800,000 to this one account. All of this was possible because I knew my organization's capabilities, my competitor's capabilities and lackadaisical approach, and convincing the buyer our program (products, services, and representation) would better suited to his organization's needs. Securing new business or converting accounts away from the competition are typically not this easy, but this would not have occurred without the competitive knowledge I was able to secure.

As you develop history in your field, you will become more aware of your competition, their sales reps and how to sell against them. For new sales reps, it is not a bad idea to keep a journal regarding the competition by company and by rep. This competitive library will help you to respond instinctively with the right questions or suggestions when facing a competitive situation.

Along with knowing your company's and competitor's capabilities, your products and services, it is also helpful to be aware of your company's history. It's always good to possess some knowledge of how your company started and / or came to be the organization they are today. Maybe it was through mergers and acquisitions, a start up from long ago, or a home-based business that found its niche. I believe it's a great idea for reps to know how their company developed and to be able to speak to that issue with customers or prospects. You can always use that to your advantage if there is a similarity between your organization and that of your customer's or prospect's. Personally, I find it fascinating to learn how major conglomerates had their humble beginnings. Nike had their beginning by a gentleman playing around with a rubber formula on a waffle iron; Kraft Foods began by Mr. J.L. Kraft selling cheese out of the back of a horse-drawn wagon.

Remember, you want to establish commonalities between you and your prospect or customer in as many areas as possible. Your common points won't guarantee a sale, but they will certainly help.

Chapter 5

Prospecting

Of all the efforts associated with the career of selling, prospecting is probably one of the least favorite. However, there are some people who relish the thought of prospecting. Those people are called hunters. They can take a stack of leads and call them as long as they can stay awake.

The other classification of sales reps is called farmers. These people can take a piece of business and grow it to its full potential. My personal opinion is the ideal rep has the ability and desire to do both. You will probably do one better than the other, but you do need to possess the ability to successfully accomplish both activities. I would compare it to be left or right handed. You are predominately either one, but you still use the other hand. However, that being said, there are organizations that are now starting to divide their sales force into hunters and farmers. They are paid differently and have different sets of qualities and expectations they are measured by. In my opinion, this is a dangerous trend, as we're losing the ability of a rep to see the sales process from a lead through to a buying customer. As a customer, I would see this process as an interruption of the pattern established to secure my business. I'm sure there are a multitude of opinions and methods to approach the hunter / farmer selling system. Hopefully you and your organization determine the best approach that ultimately puts the customer first.

Three terms to become familiar with in the realm of prospecting:

- Lead - the name of a person or organization that might possibly develop into a prospect.

- Qualifying – the act of determining whether or not a lead is able to benefit from your product or services.

- Prospect - a person or organization that can benefit from buying your product or service and has the ability to pay for it. *(Credit checks are important before moving forward.)*

Why is prospecting so important?

- Identifies those people and organizations that have a real need for your products or services.
- New Customers
- New Sales
- New Profits
- Higher commissions / bonuses
- New or additional referrals
- Keeps selling skills sharp
- Job Security

When you are qualifying leads, know if your organization has a policy governing this activity. The last thing you want to do is call a current customer or jeopardize any existing relationships or business your company currently services. Depending on your company and the product or service they represent, there are a number of methods sales territories may be divided. I've known companies to have various sales area restrictions. You should know if you have any restrictions by territory, which may be categorized by zip codes, cities, regions, and / or states. Another restriction may be that of product grouping; in which you may be able to sell the equipment but not the supplies, or just certain types of equipment. I have also heard of restrictions by industry where you are directed to target only manufacturing companies while other reps focus only on distributors or other market channels. Every organization is different based on their products, sales force capabilities, and competition. The key here is to know the guidelines before you begin the qualifying process so you are not wasting your time or possibly embarrassing your organization. Once you become familiar with the qualifying process, you are now ready to take that stack of leads and begin to gather information that will determine whether or not they are a prospect.

Before you begin to make contact with the sales lead, know your goal as to why you are contacting them. Build your message to achieve that goal. Don't wing it; anticipate potential objections or the fact that you will most likely need to leave your initial message on voice mail or e-mail. If you are selling a technical product, know the acceptable industry jargon commonly used when describing a product or service. Even though it may be your first venture at cold calling – don't sound like it! As stated in previous chapters, sound confident, knowledgeable, and positive. Every sales rep is out to save a potential customer time and / or money. I've never had a sales rep tell me otherwise. That's the premise for the call. However, make sure you have some substance to your message. If you need to leave a message on voice mail, include a "teaser" about something you have to offer that distances you from the competition, such as product quality, service, value, or enhanced image. This could obviously include a product improvement or a service that assists in identifying or controlling costs. Your primary goal for the initial call is to qualify the sales lead as a prospect and secure a second opportunity to converse with the sales lead and further match you and your organization's capabilities with the needs of the prospect.

The successful sales rep always has a prospecting system. There are a number of sales automation systems available such as ACT or Goldmine. These systems are designed to maintain your contact information as well as allow you to document your sales activities with every lead, prospect, and customer. While these systems work well, it is not mandatory to use them to guarantee success. However, these systems are excellent at providing a tool to allow you to organize your sales activities. Depending on your organizational skills, your product line, and potential customer base; you could start out with using Microsoft Office Excel or Access to document your sales activities.

So far, you are equipped with your company's prospecting do's and don'ts, a stack of sales leads, and a system to manage your qualifying activities. What's next? COURAGE and DETERMINATION.

My first thirty calls resulted in absolutely no sales, no potential sales activity, a couple of "don't ever call me again," and an absolutely defeated attitude. All of the negative thoughts came rushing into my head

- Why did I change careers? I was in control when I negotiated contracts in purchasing.
- After three months of sales training, I can't even get a "call me next week" response?
- Am I cut out to do this?
- Is this how every day is going to go?

My next stop was my sales manager's office to provide a status report on all of the appointments I just scheduled. After about five minutes of my rambling, she smiled, gave me the morning's newspaper and told me to go get a cup of coffee. After twenty minutes, we reviewed my prospecting horror story. Her assessment of my lack of success was that my expectations were too high and my voice probably had a hint of desperation as the rejections started to mount. Also, my desk was positioned in an area surrounded by some of the top sales reps in the company. While they weren't present at this time, I expected my conversations to go as smoothly as their calls to their customers. My personal expectations, given that I had a purchasing background, were to secure an appointment on two out of three calls. If you talk with most sales personnel, they all work on the ten percent rule. That is, one out of every ten calls will result in an appointment; one out of every ten appointments will result in a presentation; one out of every ten presentations will result in a new account. While I didn't like those ratios, it did take some of the pressure away from the prospecting process. It also taught me to adjust my message to various types of prospects. I took my new attitude back to my desk, made ten calls and was able to schedule three appointments and two call – backs for the following week.

There is a lot to be said for relaxing your attitude and your message. When you are desperate, you sound desperate and probably deliver your message with a tone that is less than inviting. Relaxing your tone to a level where you can project that you just want to have a conversation and possibly share some information that will improve the prospect's methods of doing business will leave a better impression with your contact. You should realize a higher level of success with this approach than "I can save you thirty percent over your current costs." Without the courage and determination to make this work, my sales career would have been short-lived. This isn't to say I didn't get that anxious feeling whenever I picked up the phone for the purpose of prospecting. I just had to take a deep breath, relax, and make that first call and secure the first appointment.

One of the most important facets of prospecting is to make sure the activity is scheduled. Block out the proper amount of time on a day that works best. This is not to say you shouldn't prospect at any other time, just know how your schedule typically works, as well as know the days and times you receive the best response. This is obviously going to vary by industry, buying behaviors, and prospecting techniques. After a few months of trying different approaches at various times, it appeared I was able to secure my best contacts and responses on Tuesday morning. My Tuesday morning would start at 5:30 as usual; don't change your schedule just because you are working out of your house. I would review my schedule, the list of prospects, and set my goal at a minimum of five appointments over the next two weeks. Obviously it was more like ten to fifteen earlier in my career when my schedule was wide open. Depending on the availability of my contacts and the responses I received, I may choose to extend the target number of appointments. Prospecting is no different than gambling – sometimes you hit it right in the first few moves, sometimes nothing works. And like the song says, "When you're hot, you're hot." You are obviously doing something right and having success at it, don't stop. These appointments are money waiting to be made.

Chapter 6

Buying Logic

Congratulations, you've secured that first appointment. Now what do you do?

Prepare to gather as much information as you possibly can to know your prospect or customer as well as possible. As I alluded to in previous chapters, the internet is a great place to gather information about any company. It's invaluable to have as much information about your client walking in the door the first time you meet with them. However, at the same time, never assume all of the information on the internet is up to date and accurate. There may have been changes in the organization structure, financial stability, or overall focus based on any number of economic factors or changing circumstances. The key to your first call is to have and/or gather as much information as possible. Confirm the important information you may already possess – they're a global manufacturer with a presence in 46 countries, they've just implemented a new warehousing system to achieve their goal of JIT deliveries, they've successfully come out of chapter 11. These are some important facts you want to know and confirm. Don't waste a buyer's time asking them to confirm they moved their manufacturing facilities from Nashville to Nogales. At this point, it doesn't matter.

The goal of your first call is to wrap your arms around the important information regarding the prospect's organization. Secondly, you want to know all of the factors involved regarding your buyer - how long have they been with the organization, where (location and/or department) did they begin working, what are their goals for the product or service you are selling? Learn as much as you can about their personality and buying behavior so you can compile an effective proposal and presentation. Also give consideration to all of the buyer's needs. Look around their work area or office. What do you see with regards to their personal life – pictures of kids; pictures of them fishing, golfing, or their favorite car;

awards for performance or association certifications? These can lead to great conversation topics. However, don't go on about a subject you have little knowledge of for risk of losing credibility. Also, while you're scanning their office for personal info, look around for competitive information. Scan the office for competitor's catalogs, private label brands only distributed by the competition, any boxes with your competitor's labels. You don't need to go through the office like it's a garage sale, but casually compliment your prospect on their work area while at the same time perusing the desk, walls, and bookcase for conversation pieces or competitive information. If their work area is a disaster zone, you may just mention in a humorous way that it looks like they have a lot on their plate. Either way, people like to comment on their space. One prospect I called on had very little in the way of personal information displayed about him except for a 3 X 5 picture of him holding a fish. I know very little about fishing, but casually asked where he caught the fish. Thirty minutes later I had info on the family tree, the last three cars he owned, and the fact he was the head of a local association which also could use my services. On the surface, this person and I had very little in common. By just showing a little bit of interest on a personal level helped secure a $100,000 account and another $10,000 order for his association. As I've said before, people buy from people they like. Develop the relationship and you have the ability to gain the edge over your competition.

Learn the differences in your buyers. It's very important to know their backgrounds – where did they come from, how did they get to where they are now? All the while they are talking you should be taking mental notes, which you need to write down immediately after the meeting. Don't write their personal information while they are talking or they are going to think you're writing a book about them. As they are speaking, listen for commonalities with your background. Did you grow up in the same area? Did you attend the same college? Are they married and do they have children? In my world, I referred to this as points of connectivity. The more common points you have, the easier it could or should be to develop and maintain the relationship.

Learn their sets of values. What do they consider important? Are they looking only for the best price? Do they understand the price / value concept? What are their expectations from a sales representative? What do they like or dislike about their current vendor for your product or service? What improvements would they like to see? In short, learn as much about their buying logic as they are willing to share. As an example, I had a prospect who was very egocentric. He never wanted to be questioned on the way he did business and always wanted to be treated as though he was the most important customer. In his world, everything was an emergency; it was just his way of doing business. And if you ever expected a thank you for going out of your way for him, you would be grossly disappointed. Lucky for me, he was buying from the competition and I knew that sales rep would not put up with this scenario for more than a couple of orders. After my first meeting with him, I told him I understood he was buying from our competitor, but if he ever needed something our competitor couldn't deliver, I would be there for him. Within a month, I had him out for a facility tour and two weeks later had all of the business. My pricing was within 3% of my competitor and our products were basically the same as we were both in the distribution business. The competitive difference was my tolerance level. I took the time to get to know the buyer's background and knew he viewed life from a self-made pedestal. Armed with that information, it was easy to manage that account. The interesting thing is I didn't do anything more for him than I did for my other key accounts. I just did it in a way that made him feel special.

Along those lines, it's important to learn if the buyer applies their set of values consistently across the board. Do they approach purchases of MRO products the same as they would a capitol purchase – machinery, furniture, major assets, etc.? Some buyers would request pricing from me for products outside of the normal realm and because of my relationship, I would get the last look at the pricing if I was competitive. In the case of the previously mentioned buyer, he would buy whatever I could sell him. If he had a need for something that wasn't in my catalog, he would call me to see if I could source the product for him. It was all about making his life easy. I was more than glad to accommodate.

Let's review instinctive buying. As we know in life, the basic needs are food, shelter, and sleep. All three are necessary to get you through life. You may be able to survive without one or the other for a short period of time, but eventually that basic need will become the next thing you seek. Businesses and organizations are no different. Every company I have ever worked for or with, has displayed a basic set of needs. There are basic operational needs – utilities, equipment, operational supplies, and appropriate personnel. Much like the human body will not survive for any substantial period of time without food; organizations will not survive without the very basic needs that keep it in operation. Knowing how your product or service fit into your customer's organization is vital in determining your importance to the client. What's more important to an airlines – jet fuel or office supplies? What's more important to a direct mail company – check processing equipment / credit card verification services or a file cabinet? In essence, all are needed to maintain an efficient operation. However, without jet fuel an airline is out of business as is a direct mail company without the proper equipment to process orders and payments. The message here is to know where you and your product or service fit into your client's food chain. How are you going to match your customer's needs with your offering? How are you going to distinguish your offering from their current source as well as other competitors? Knowing your customer's behaviors now becomes an important piece of the puzzle as to how you move forward to develop the relationship. Much like the buyer mentioned in the previous paragraph whose basic need was to feel important and unchallenged; all buyers have some basic needs and behaviors. Some like to operate like a Turkish market where everything is negotiable, some like to delegate part of their work to you, and some like to keep you on edge by never letting you get comfortable with the business relationship. The key is to respect the buyer's position along with their basic instincts. Your challenge is to determine a method of satisfying those basic instincts to gain their trust and the business, without mortgaging yours or your company's business practices or ethics.

Once you get through the efforts spent on determining how you and your company's products fit into the client's world, you then need to address their logic for purchasing whatever it is you're selling. Are they or why are they considering your product and why should they buy it from you and not your competitor? Obviously the client is spending the time meeting with you to look at potential solutions and opportunities for your product to fit into their organization, so get to the subject at hand. What is their logic or motivation to review your product line? Are they dissatisfied with their current source, do they feel they are currently over paying, or are they just trying to stay in touch with all solutions that may be available? Depending on your product or service, the list could go on. The key here is to know why you are there and what actions you can take to convince the buyer to advance the sales process. As a buyer I was very upfront as to whether I was gathering information for a future purchase or addressing an immediate need. Once you determine their logic for buying, you are on your way to define your next actions as to how you proceed in developing the sales presentation and strategy.

There are various theories of buying motivation. First, let's begin with the rational motivators:

> Pricing – When it comes to dollars and cents, this is an easy motivator. Most children know that $58 is less than $65. If price is the only criteria the buyer is measuring their purchase on, this is an easy motivator to address. However the important factor here is the unknown. Is the buyer evaluating an actual item or a product concept? Are you being asked to submit a price on the specific product number ABC123, which the buyer has already identified as the solution to their needs? Or are you being asked to submit a price on a product concept that is left up to you to determine the specific item that will solve the buyer's requirements? If a buyer identifies a specific product, you can supply the price for that item. At the same time to build your

relationship, if allowed to, you may suggest alternative products that could either save them additional money and / or improve the value of their purchase. Any sales rep that answers the price question with only a number is completely missing the boat. The price question affords you the opportunity to display your ability to become a consultant on the customer's behalf and not just another bid in the file. Never confuse price for value. Price is the monetary cost of the item; value is the benefit(s) you and your product or services provide.

Reliability – A customer is familiar with a particular product or service and is satisfied that it will serve their needs. This is a good factor to sell as part of the price / value relationship. Is the item the buyer requests as reliable as other competitive items or services on the market? If it is an item that is purchased on a once-every-three-years basis you should consider addressing any applicable technology changes that may have occurred since their last purchase.

Durability – This is a key factor to address when products have a perceived life expectancy. As the saying goes, "perception is reality." If a customer has the option of a few different product solutions, durability is an issue that needs to be addressed. This is the area where the interviewing skills need to succinctly identify customer expectations. As an example, let's look at a piece of warehouse equipment – the forklift. Criteria that needs to be evaluated such as how often is it used, warehouse ceiling height, and maximum weight load are just a few bits of information a materials handling sales rep will need to know before suggesting the right equipment options in addressing the durability requirement. Again, the price / value conversation needs to occur so the buyer's equipment durability expectations or value are met and are in line with the price of the product.

Length of Effective Use – This primarily applies to machinery and equipment. Does anyone actually purchase office copiers anymore? With all of the constant technology changes and capabilities, I would be hard pressed to see why any organization would purchase a high-volume multi-purpose copier. When I first started working, copiers were larger than a Volkswagen and only provided copies. Fast forward to today when copiers are about one-third the size and can scan, e-mail, print booklets in color, and improve the quality of the original. That's just one example regarding length of effective use. When selling any type of equipment or machinery with moving parts, you should address this topic as it could be a competitive difference that hopefully works in your favor.

Another set of buying motivators relate to emotions. Let's review some of the emotional motivators.

Security – A buyer wants to know that they made a safe decision for their organization. Depending on the product, they may take a calculated risk. However, if the item affects the finished product of their company they are less likely to take that risk without sound reasoning. If you're selling the "safe" product, your challenge is somewhat minimized depending on your competition. However, if you're offering the "calculated risk" solution, you may need to surround it with guarantees or warrantees.

Comfort – Some buyers want to make their decision on what makes them comfortable. Depending on the item, this may be the most logical option. However, as a sales rep, if your product or service is not the "comfortable" choice, it is your responsibility to set the stage as to why your product or service could ultimately become the comfortable choice. Depending on your product or service, this is typically a longer sales cycle as buyers typically don't have an urgency to change sources. Be creative – get your foot in the door, keep subtle reminders in front of the buyer that you're there in an emergency. One October I called a lead to see if we could schedule an introduction meeting. The buyer informed me they review and award their business annually every September. My first thought was *"that's a good line to get rid of a sales person."* Instead of putting them in the long term prospect file, I made a note in my calendar to drop off information on the first Tuesday of every month at 10:00. The information packet consisted of a sell sheet on one of our services along with a product sample of an item I thought they would use on a daily basis or something I felt the competitor had not shown them.

In the first information packet I had a cover letter explaining my intentions which were to empathize with the buyer that time was valuable and her review process for my products and services was eleven months away. However, in the interim, she would be receiving these monthly information packets that she could read at her leisure that would inform her about our company and the benefits of employing us as their supplier. The first Tuesday of every month at 10:00 I personally delivered my information packet. By the fourth month the receptionist just started laughing and reset her watch because she knew it was 10:00 on the dot. *Voila* – The eleventh month I entered the reception area only to find the buyer waiting for me. I was a little surprised when she asked if I had time to for a quick meeting. After settling into her office, she thanked me for my professionalism and respecting her time. She never had a vendor take this approach before. She handed me the request for quotation for her supplies and we scheduled the next meeting. She informed me if I was competitive, I would get the business. Through the monthly information packets, she became very familiar with our services and informed me no formal presentation was required. Within a week, I was converting a two hundred and fifty thousand dollar account. The point of this story was the buyer became comfortable with me through a non-threatening or non-confrontational approach. She became comfortable with me and my organization.

Ego – See the earlier paragraphs in this chapter. Some buyers want to make their own decision. They don't want to always make the comfortable decision, but have a desire to make changes or decisions for purely selfish reasons. If faced with a buyer who makes ego-driven decisions, you need to know how you can make them look good. The sale is no longer primarily focused on product, pricing, and service. It is now focused on an entire new set of values. The key here is to load up on open probes and get the buyer talking about themselves so you can determine how to feed their ego by choosing your product or service. There is a very fine line to walk in this situation. When faced with this situation, I always tried to find out if they belonged to either a buyer's or industry association. From there I would try to establish some commonalities. These could be people we may both know, similar organizations I've sold to, and associations where both of our companies may have memberships. I'm sure you can think of others as well. The approach here is to focus on the buyer from a personal standpoint, but make sure business is a close second. When the buyer's decisions work in your favor, it's fantastic. When they work against you, it's frustrating but opens the door to another challenge.

These are just a few examples of buying logic from a rational and emotional perspective. Aside from the motivators, another reason people buy is to solve a problem. It could be as simple as replenishing coffee supplies for the office to something as critical as a part for a machine required in producing their key product. This is where it is very important for you as a sales rep to know how you can penetrate an account to help them solve their purchasing needs. As an example, your company sells and distributes general maintenance supplies for factories and offices. One of your customers has a need for warehousing of other maintenance supplies you do not sell. You could enhance your status as a supplier to this customer by offering one of two solutions; determine if you can source comparable products for them or offer the solution of inventorying those customer specified items for them and delivering them along with your products. Making the buyer's life easier is just one additional way to build the relationship and at the same time make it more difficult for your customer to convert to a new supplier.

A common theme in all of the buyer logic and motivation topics is that of knowing the buyer, as well as how does the buyer perceive themselves? In life, there is the ideal situation and then there's reality. Most people have hopes or visions of whom or what they want to be, which you could classify as an ideal situation or a dream. The reality is what you have actually become. Sometimes people are living the dream, sometimes they are not. Buyers are no different. They have a sense of self-concept. Their *self-assessment* tells them what they really think they are – a buyer of general maintenance services for a shopping mall. Their *embellished self-assessment* tells them how they would like to think of themselves – without my input and control the shopping mall would not be able to operate. There is also another side of self-concept and that is the "other" side. Their *external perception* relates to how they perceive that other people perceive them. In other words, a buyer may feel that sales reps see them as a challenge or hard-nosed buyer that always has reps knowing they need to do their homework to gain this buyer's business. The *embellished external perception* relates to how the buyer would like to have others perceive them. The buyer might like to think others see them as a fair business partner who is enjoyable to be around. The reason they attend social events together is because they are viewed as someone likeable, not as a way to "buy" their business. This is very critical information to know. If you can quickly and sincerely appeal to the buyer's sense of self, you've just broken down another barrier and added another positive reason for the buyer to work with you.

Now for the flipside to everything in the previous paragraph, here are some of the challenges you may face even though you've identified the self-concept of a buyer:

The buyer is not realistic in their assessment of their self-concept. They fluctuate in their self-assessment and external perception. Their views are in a constant state of flux. This could be affected by both work and personal issues. Some indicators are constantly changing agendas – one day they are in agreement with most everything you propose, the next day everything has changed. When this becomes a consistent behavior, be very careful to document any and all changes. At some point this becomes a shell game that you can win with excellent documentation, organizational skills, and an unflappable personality.

Much like the above example, the buyer changes the embellished self-assessment or external perception. Their embellished self-assessment changes to an unrealistic self-assessment and they view themselves as virtually infallible. A couple possible reasons behind this change could be related to their status within the company or a change in either their business or personal life that has made them insecure. This could lead to the need to exert ultimate control over situations that remain in their realm. Again, documentation and getting to "why" is very important in this scenario as well. Remember, the less input or control you have in a sales situation, the more you need to sharpen your sales skills.

Believe it or not, sometimes no matter how well in touch a buyer is with themselves, they do feel guilt over a possible purchase. Sometimes a sales rep can deliver their best presentation with all of the reasons a buyer should upgrade into the next generation of software, equipment, furniture, or whatever only to hear the buyer fell back to a position of "what we use now is acceptable." Case in point, I worked for a direct mail firm located in the downtown area of a major city. The operation encompassed seven floors of an office building. Four of the seven floors housed clerical operations requiring constant movement of documents, checks, and equipment. The only way to accomplish this paper shuffle was the freight elevator, of which there was only one.

The building was built in 1929, so we are not working with state of the art equipment here. We hired a time and motion consultant to evaluate what our operation was really costing us versus if we relocated to a one-story building out in the near suburbs. The study results showed we were really paying in excess of two and a half times the rent costs as a result of lost production, we could have reduced our staff by an estimated 15%, and finally we could have reduced our rent by an estimated $2.00 per square foot. I met with the consultant to make sure the fluff was eliminated from the numbers and we went conservative across the board. The savings were still astronomical and easily quantifiable. The decision from the president – "I like the restaurants and the lakefront, I would rather stay here." All the sound reasoning in the world sometimes cannot overcome self-serving reasoning.

We have just spent a little bit of time looking into the buyer's mind and how it potentially works. Now let's look at the motivational analysis of the prospect. First thing to do when you visit your prospect's place of business is to look at the environment. As an example, let's say you're selling facility management services. You visit two offices, one has stained partitions that aren't aligned, missing light diffusers, phone cords and computer cables extended over partitions, mis-matched furniture and in general is poorly designed. The second office is well lit; everything appears organized and well planned. After the initial introductions, general benefits statement, and questions related to their need and goal for your services, it would be wise to inquire about other purchases made related to your product or service line(s.) Are they or have they worked with a competitor, if so, inquire about their level of satisfaction with the competitor. This open probe usually lends itself to gathering critical information in knowing how to structure your offering and presentation. The information you gather will also indicate whether you are or are not a good fit for this prospect. Further inquire about the buying habits of this prospect – are they focused on staying on top of technological changes or do they only review upgrades when their systems become obsolete? This will tell you if this is an ongoing project or one-time sale. Lastly, attempt to have the buyer share their opinion of other firms or products they may have experienced. Again, this will provide a good indicator of likes and dislikes you can apply to your presentation.

Keep the two aforementioned offices in mind as we go through the next paragraphs of buying motives, talking points, and finally, the presentation.

You're in the process of preparing your presentation. You have all of the materials you need to surround and sell your product or service. Now comes the fun part – how do you use and deliver these materials to paint a picture for the buyer where they can see themselves using the goods you are selling? Here is where we look at buying motives versus talking points. A talking point is just that – a tangible product or service where you describe the features and benefits. These talking points have qualities that are measurable. A buying motive goes back to the concepts we discussed in the previous paragraphs of how you get to paint a picture in the buyer's mind of why they would have a desire to purchase this product or service.

Let's go back to the previous example of the rep selling facility management services. The first office is unsightly, unorganized, and generally gives the impression of a chaotic atmosphere. However, during the initial interview, the sales rep uncovered the fact this company has only been in business for a couple of years and assumed their office space in an "as is" condition. They have grown their sales and are now looking to revamp their facilities.

This is a great opportunity because the talking points are fairly obvious – operational requirements for equipment and work flow, potential technology improvements, and general ambiance likes and dislikes. The buying motives would be how the buyer envisions the office appearance as well as their goal for how the office functions. How will your redesign of the facility and change in processes have a positive impact on the bottom line? This is where you need to know their ultimate goals and paint the picture in your presentation where they can see how the changes will meet their needs on all levels. The second office example, while it appears to offer less challenges, may ultimately present just as many challenges. While the facility appears to be presentable, the way in which they operate and potentially use old technology may be costing them more money that could easily be justified with some revisions. On the surface, it would be very easy to assume that the first customer probably could not afford or would not have an interest in making required changes and that the second customer would need very little in the way of change. However, both scenarios address the importance of learning as much about your customer as they'll allow.

Done right, both examples offer a great opportunity for talking points as well as learning their buying motives and satisfying those in your presentation. Another thing to keep in mind when developing and delivering your presentation, address the points in the order of importance to your customer. Don't go in easy to difficult or least expensive to most expensive order. Grab that buyer's attention by marrying your presentation with their priorities. You will have a more inter-active presentation as well as eliminate the chance of going off on a tangent about a small meaningless item. I always operated under the premise of I'll never have more of their attention than I do at the beginning of a presentation.

Chapter 7

Essentials for the Initial Interview

Congratulations, you have reached the first plateau on the road to success. Your courage and determination have paid off; you have secured your first meeting. Now what do you do?

It is now time to structure the agenda for your first sales call to the prospect. Review your notes from your initial communication with the prospect. Was there a certain point in the discussion that triggered the prospect to schedule the appointment? Whatever the catalyst that served as a reason for securing the meeting should be included in the agenda for your initial meeting.

Now it's time for you to gather a little background information. In this day and age of the internet, gathering information on a prospect is a lot easier than ever. You have the ability to research the prospective company, key personnel, mission statements, financials, as well as any other details that may give you insight or help establish commonalities between both of your organizations. The obvious place to start is on the prospect's website to gather as much information as they are willing to share. Additional information may be obtained through websites such as Hoover's www.hoovers.com or Dun & Bradstreet www.dnb.com. These websites offer information on company financials and key personnel in the event the company's website does not offer this data. Some of these websites provide a brief overview and require a subscription to obtain additional data. You may also check LinkedIn for additional company news, although it may be somewhat limited. However, LinkedIn would be an excellent source to gather information regarding your contact. LinkedIn focuses more on the business side, where as Facebook could provide insight to their personal side. A word of caution – make sure the person you are looking at is the exact match as your contact. While it's always nice to know a little bit about the person across the desk, it could be dangerous if you look at the wrong profile and assume it's your contact. Be very cautious as to how and when you use this information. Sometimes no information is better than bad information.

The first meeting is usually interesting and unique. It's almost like a friendly chess match. Body language is just as important as oral communication. As we discussed in earlier chapters, be knowledgeable, be professional; and most of all – be on time. Again, on time is defined as walking into the customer's facility ten minutes prior to your appointment. I've never heard of anyone losing business because they were ten minutes early.

Assuming there isn't an immediate need, the goal of the first call should be to establish that you and your organization have the products, services, and solutions for the prospect's requirements. To accomplish that goal, you'll need to ask some questions that require lengthy answers as well as questions that require a "yes" or "no" response. In sales terms, these are referred to as open and closed probes. An open probe requires an answer that explains something in detail. A closed probe would be a question requiring a simple yes or no response. The key is to get the prospect to provide as much information as possible about themselves and their organization that will allow you to develop a presentation to meet or exceed their needs. In my purchasing experience, too often sales reps would want to tell me all about their product or service and how much cheaper they were than the competition. Or, another approach was to provide a list of services they thought I needed before they ever qualified my needs. These services had to increase their cost to do business, which provided me with the opportunity to negotiate better pricing with them since I didn't require most of the services they were offering. Of course I waited until I received their formal price quotation then began the negotiation from there. A simple lesson is do not give away the house when all the prospect wants is a tent. You will have the ability to upsell value-added services later and potentially increase your sales and profits.

The initial questions after the general small talk about the weather or current local events should be related to the organization:

- First of all, always, always, always deliver your general benefits statement. This statement defines the purpose behind your visit. It can be something like, "the purpose of my visit today is to review your processes for ……. and see how we can assist you in identifying and eliminating hidden costs……." Make sure you get confirmation that the buyer agrees on the purpose for your visit and doesn't have you or your company confused with another vendor. I wouldn't be saying that if it didn't happen.

- How long has the organization been in business?

- How is it structured

    - Locations
    - Employees
    - Divisions
    - Any community service initiatives they may have listed on their website

- Short and long term goals if they are relevant to your product or service.

Even though you may have all of this information from the company's website, it's always good to confirm the details as well as determine how much your buyer knows about their organization.

The next set of questions should focus on the buyer or decision maker.

- How long have you been with the company?
- What are their current responsibilities?
- Have they held any other positions within the organization?
- Have they worked at any other organizations? (This information could be valuable for acquiring new prospects.)
- What is their past experience?

As you are asking these questions, which are typically all open probes, make sure you are capturing their answers as a reference point to better develop your presentation should relevant information need to be included. It also shows that you feel their response is important enough to take note of for future reference. For the sake of being courteous, always ask the buyer if they mind that you take notes while they talk.

Once you've gathered the necessary information to advance to the next step of the sales process and the next meeting, you should focus your next set of questions on their needs or current mode of operation and how your organization could provide the solution for those requirements. This is where your questions become more product or service focused along with using open and closed probes. This would also be the place where you would include the question(s) discussed on your initial communication that triggered the buyer to schedule the meeting with you. Design these questions to not only determine the prospect's needs, but also highlight the strengths of your organization.

As an example, a customer uses five styles of widgets in their operation. However, two of the widgets are seasonal. You uncover the fact that their current source requires a special order for the seasonal widgets, which requires a lengthy lead time, as well as a 50% pre-payment. You know that your company has the ability to either inventory the seasonal widgets or pre-schedule production runs of these items. At this stage you may want to ask the obvious question, "If we could deliver a solution that would reduce or eliminate the lead time and pre-payment, would you consider using my organization as a source?" This question is known as a trial close; we'll review trial closes and their importance in further detail in chapter 13.

You will either receive a "yes" response or additional information that the current widget supplier offers other services that offsets the challenges for securing the seasonal widgets. Always get to the entire story or situation before you make an assumption that could embarrass you in the presentation process. As a new sales rep, you may listen to the challenges the prospect encountered while trying to acquire the seasonal widgets and assume your solution would be an improvement, only to find out there are other factors involved that might make this situation a little more palatable with their current source.

As you progress through your list of questions, always confirm your understanding of the buyer's responses. You don't need to confirm every response immediately, but you should, at the very least, summarize your assessment of the buyer's requirements and their current situation after the Q & A part of the meeting is coming to a close.

At the same time, a good decision maker will also have an agenda with some questions about you and your organization. Be certain you are prepared to answer those questions. In my purchasing days, I always had key points to review with any new vendor. Depending on the product or service I was reviewing, I never wanted to waste a vendor's time with little or vague information. If a decision maker does not provide accurate information, there is no way they can expect a relevant response that will be of any value to them or their organization. Make note of anyone who doesn't have an agenda, list of questions, or someone who displays only a casual interest in the process. In the event you witness these behaviors, be prepared for one of two scenarios:

- Either the buyer has nothing better to do than fill their day with meetings (this is not a joke, there are buyers who schedule meetings with sales reps to fill their day with activity,) there are also companies that require buyers to fill a quota of meetings with sales reps.

- This buyer wants to be sold. This isn't a bad situation; you will just need to work a little harder. Thorough preparation will help overcome an indifferent buyer. Coming to the initial interview with the information you gathered about the company and the buyer gives you an advantage in developing a more targeted list of questions.

> The best way to overcome indifference and get to the reason you are being considered as a source is through open probes. In this situation, you need to get the buyer to respond to your questions with in depth information of their likes and dislikes of their current situation related to their vendor, service, and / or product(s.)

Early in my sales career I called on our local PBS station. My contact was pleasant but quickly got to the point that she was not looking for another source for our products. I said I understood and went off to some small talk about her having the same last name as a former business contact and was she related to him. She said she also dealt with his company, but was not a relative. Out of the blue, she responded with an "oh come on in anyway and let's see what you have to offer." However, she said to keep in mind that they were very satisfied with their current source and did not anticipate a change. I thanked her for the opportunity and said I looked forward to earning her business.

The day of the meeting I was escorted to the buyer's desk. We exchanged the usual greetings and were about to begin our meeting. As I was about to sit down, the buyer reinforced her message that she didn't anticipate a change in vendors. My response was that I understood her position and if I couldn't uncover ways to not only save money but improve her process of securing the products, then my company should not be considered as a potential supplier. The meeting went well and we agreed to a formal presentation of our products and services within a two week timeframe. In my interview I didn't uncover any surprises as to products required as part of their daily operation, nor did they require any special services that would pose a challenge.

That being said, I began to do my homework on my competition. My contact shared the name of her current source on my initial phone call, so I knew who I was competing with for the business. Ironically, at one point in my purchasing career, I used this very company as a back-up source to my primary supplier. Two things I knew about this company is they were not the cheapest on the block, nor did they like to serve as a back-up supplier. At one point, the owner of this company actually called me to say they wanted to function as my primary supplier or no longer work with us. That was one trial close that did not work in his favor. I wished him well and said we may cross paths again. Little did we know it would be as his competitor. I was also aware that his inventory levels were nowhere near that of my company. Add it all up and this should be a slam dunk for me – not really. My job now is to structure my presentation based on the feedback received during my initial interview and highlight the buyer's priorities, along with accenting our strengths versus her current supplier's weaknesses, without mentioning her current source by name.

Two weeks later I was making the presentation of all places, in the cafeteria. The conference rooms were full and the buyer wanted to get away from the distractions of her work area. Luckily, it was during the time of day when the cafeteria had little traffic. However, there was still the occasional distraction. This was definitely a lesson in how to focus on the matter at hand and tune out the activities around me. Presentation activities and challenges will be discussed later in Chapter 11 and 12.

The presentation went well, very interactive, which shows the buyer comprehended and filtered the information that was shared. With the presentation and summary complete, I went into my closing statement of "if we / would you?" My buyer's response was that she liked everything she heard regarding services and account management. She promised to review the pricing and get back to me within the next two to three weeks.

One side note about me is I am not a very patient person. Hearing two to three weeks sounded like two to three years. Knowing full well that I did everything I could to that point, I thanked her for her time and promised to contact her in a couple of weeks to see if there were any follow up issues that needed further clarification. She said that would be fine and we parted ways. By the end of the week, I had a message that an order was waiting for me at their reception area. Picking up orders was not my typical mode of operation, but I was young, hungry, and competitive. I knew by picking up the order, that would separate me from the competition. That account stayed with me until I left the industry some thirteen years later.

In summary, your first interview is going to be your last chance to make a first impression. You worked hard to get to this stage. Make sure you covered all of your bases to get to the next step of the sales phase.

Chapter 8

The Art of Persuasion

Now, you have completed the initial interview and have reached the point that you have uncovered a few of the hot buttons expressed as deal breakers. That is great information to have to build that next step in convincing your buyer that you have the solutions to their needs.

Too often people confuse persuasion with trying to convince people of agreeing to something they would normally resist. Successful persuasion is based on knowing the background of the situation, knowing or uncovering goals of your contact and their organization, then recommending a solution to everyone's satisfaction. Where sales reps typically fail at the art of persuasion is either not knowing all of the relevant facts and goals or only focusing on their perceived ability to solve the issue on their terms without any consideration for the customer.

I'll use my first large account I secured as an example. One of our sales reps retired and I was given one of his average accounts. The good news was that they were buying from us; the bad news is we were only getting approximately five percent of their total business. Although the first appointment was easy to secure, this was basically a new account given our limited activity and poor perception the buyer expressed regarding our former rep and the company. Basically, in baseball terms, I'm a pinch hitter coming in with an 0 and 2 count. Great opportunity at hand; either do all the right things and secure a large account or talk about what could have been. Preparation for this call was going to be tantamount to my success. Chances are that without something to show that I would be a different rep and bring some value to the relationship; this was going to be my last visit to this client.

Once we got through the general benefits statement and small talk, my plan was to dive right in and address the issues they buyer expressed over the phone that related to his relationship with the former rep and the poor impression of my organization. My thoughts were that if I could not overcome these two issues, the balance of the meeting was going to be a real challenge. If or when I got beyond those two issues, my focus was going to be on what basis did the buyer feel our competitor met or exceeded his expectations and why, which would lead into the buyer's priorities.

By today's standards, I went into this account blind. The internet was yet to be invented and the former rep's files had a couple of cryptic notes that were as helpful as yesterday's weather report. The only information of any value was an old price list, which in reviewing it, provided my first clue as to one of the issues. The former rep's account run consisted primarily of small to mid-sized accounts. Instead of becoming aggressive with the large account and pricing them competitively, he gave then the same pricing as a mid-sized account because that was the level of their purchases. Mistake number one, but good for me.

The day has finally arrived for what could be a major career building sales call. I drove into the large campus setting filled with two story buildings and completely filled parking lots in the middle of what seemed to be a forest. This setting just doubled the importance of securing the majority of this business. I was thoroughly prepared for this call and there wasn't any room in improvement. All of my bases were covered as I knew exactly what I was going to say based upon the initial responses. All of my questions focused on the buyer's priorities. My ultimate goal was to convert the business at this meeting; my secondary goal was to develop a corrective action plan that would allow for subsequent meetings. Failure to achieve either of these goals was not an option.

I'm escorted up to the buyer's office where I receive a surprising warm welcome. We took a brief tour of the facilities, where I was able to go into the open and closed probes about the company and his responsibilities. A customer facility tour is a great opportunity if it ever presents itself. We grabbed a quick cup of coffee and went back to his office. I delivered my general benefits statement, to which he agreed and we progressed to the series of open probes respective to the relationship and his priorities. All of the responses appeared to be straight forward and sincere. I've never had a buyer give me all of the information I was looking for in one response. I'm always prepared to read through some double-speak, jargons, or double entendre. My questions were either right on target or this buyer was making my job easy. At the same time my subsequent questions would almost seem like I'm baiting him for answers that were very apparent, so I went into a trial close. "In looking at the facilities and the people count, there is obviously a disconnect between the orders we receive versus the opportunity. What do we need to do to earn more of your business?" As I'm speaking these words, I'm praying that I read the situation correctly and I'm not making a huge mistake. What a relief, the buyer just started laughing. He said nobody was ever that straight forward with him, and not missing a beat, he went into his top three priorities for gaining additional business. The priorities were – consistent representation, which meant scheduled weekly visits; review pricing on his top 50 items used in the daily operation; and for my company to provide a dummy terminal to allow him to place his orders on line at his convenience. I immediately agreed to all of his requests and scheduled our weekly meetings for 10:00 every Wednesday. The following week; our terminal was installed and the competitor's was removed and we reviewed the revised price list and only needed to make a couple of minor adjustments. In our first year of doing business, we increased the sales from $50,000 to $625,000. Ultimately, they became a million dollar plus account for the company.

Now you might say, "What persuasive techniques did you use?" Let's go back and breakdown the stages of this sales call. Here's what I knew about this account prior to my first visit:

- Pricing was not competitive
- Customer had a poor impression of the former rep and our company
- We only received five percent of the estimated business
- Large account with a huge potential

My preparation for that first call centered around gathering information to become familiar with the organization as well as the buyer. As I previously alluded to, the internet was just a dream which meant I needed to physically hunt down any information available about this account. Secondly, I needed to uncover the reasons behind the negative feelings towards the former rep and my organization. I knew that if I could gather that knowledge, I could build a presentation that would definitely increase our business with this customer / prospect.

I'm a firm believer in the fact that sometimes the stars line up correctly and the gods smile down on you. Some people would call this luck, kismet, karma or whatever. I'm also a firm believer that you create your own luck as in making the right first impression that served as an entrée into a facility tour. I couldn't have asked for a better scenario. Walking around their office allowed me to easily identify my competitor as they had a unique private label brand only they distributed. I immediately knew the challenges I would face as a result of my competitor's strengths and knew exactly which weaknesses to target depending on my buyer's priorities. Of course, I needed to address our dirty laundry prior to reviewing the competition. Additionally, the facilities tour gave me a chance to see how the buyer interacted with the rest of their personnel. It became very apparent that he loved being acknowledged as he walked through the various areas. Based on our initial conversation, it was clear that image along with doing the job the right way were very high on his vendor priority list. Knowing this buyer had an ego that liked to be stroked gave me the foresight as to how to position the features and benefits of dealing with me and my company.

While I succeeded in overcoming the initial two challenges within the first two visits, it was over the next four weeks where I spoon-fed product ideas as well as suggested operational changes that not only reduced his costs along with improving my margins; but also consolidated his purchases to increase his order size and reduce my company's operational costs in servicing this customer. One of the persuasive techniques used to accomplish this was by providing samples of products that were equal in quality to the items he was using, but had a better cost structure. My approach was to always get his approval that the alternate product was acceptable, we would then discuss the savings in terms of the item as well as projected annual savings based on his annual purchases over the past twelve months. He obviously provided this data as we were just building our business with his account. The increase in order size was tied to us providing a terminal and printer at no charge. We provided this not only to convert the majority of the business from the competitor, but also gained agreement that he would place his primary order on Wednesday. The reason we selected Wednesday is that it was the slowest day of the week for our warehouse staff. The first four weeks we had classic the "If we/would you," conversations every visit. Subsequently, at the end of every meeting, he arrived at a better way to purchase our products and distribute them throughout his operation, and we continued to increase our business.

The ultimate scenario was when we began to discuss special products – those not kept in inventory in the warehouse. For these items, we would need to write a separate request for pricing from the manufacturer or alternate source, get the profit margin approved by a manager, and finally, place the order through our purchasing department. My competitor had a much simpler way of processing specials, which ultimately made it easier for the customer. The bottom line was the process I had to work with could easily take a week just to get an answer, while my competitor's process could take less than a day. Again, the persuasive technique was making my customer's mode of operation easier and that is exactly how I presented my proposal. Let's sit down and identify those consistently used special items. We can obtain a cost, lock it in for ninety days and process orders immediately versus the back and forth with my competitor. If the volumes were high enough, we could even bring them into our warehouse as a proprietary item which he could just add to his normal order. Basically, all I did was take our weakness and turn it into a strength to combat the competition's system, which initially was better than ours.

The key in all of this was knowing that if I made the buyer's job easier and made him look good, I would have an easier time persuading him to make future changes to products, pricing, or services.

To enhance your persuasive skills, you need to help your customer visualize the benefits of the purchase. As an example, you have a customer who specifies a certain computer supply that they have purchased over the years for a unit cost of $10.00. You are aware of a similar product, that could easily save the customer 15%, or $1.50 per unit. It would be easy; and probably at the same time, a mistake to walk into your buyer's office and say "I have a product that can save you some money." Two things wrong with that message are, it doesn't quantify the savings; and it also makes it sound as though the buyer hasn't been doing his homework. To help the buyer visualize your message, you may want to say, "In reviewing your purchases, I believe I've uncovered an opportunity to explore which could result in realistic measurable savings for your operation. I found the proverbial widget that would save 15% per unit or, based on your actual annual purchases, fifty five hundred dollars per year. My proposal would be to test a few of these in your daily operation to make sure the quality meets your expectations. Can I bring those by next week or should I have them sent to your attention?" A couple of improvements in the message are that you are helping the buyer see the ultimate benefit along with the fact you are willing to test the widget to make sure they are of satisfactory quality. You have just painted the picture of no risk, all reward. You are no longer talking about one dollar and fifty cents, but a stack of fifty five hundred George Washington's. This proposal suggestion works whether it's related to staffing, man hours, salary, cost per unit, etc. Maximize the benefit, minimize the risk.

Persuasion is not about winning an argument. Persuasion is matching your capabilities with the customer's needs and leading them down the path so the customer agrees the solution is in their best interest.

Chapter 9

The Presentation – Basics

When constructing your presentation, you must first identify the purpose. Is your presentation to close the deal or get to the next step in the decision process?

As an example, in my purchasing days, my organization was looking for an architect firm for purposes of redesigning and constructing current and new office space. Under normal conditions, that shouldn't be too difficult a task. However, we were located in a building in downtown Chicago that was built in 1929. There was a myriad of challenges in this building that modern construction did not pose, so hiring the right architect was extremely important for this project. The process was to interview various firms until we agreed on three firms who impressed us as having the capabilities and mindset to develop and manage this project. The first presentation by all of the firms we interviewed was providing us a capabilities assessment of their firm. This included their key personnel, their experience, major or similar construction projects managed by their firm, and lastly a general overview of their rate schedule. This presentation was fairly informal, and was designed to be that way. We were looking for the basic information to determine who should go to the next step. Of the initial six firms, we selected three to come back for a second interview and presentation.

This second round of presentations would address additional details such as the architecture firm's experience with examples of projects of working in old buildings, challenges they encountered along with the resolutions, the bidding process with contractors and sub-contractors, project management, and all of the other "what ifs" along the way that could potentially arise. This was more of a formal presentation with actual visuals and details provided. Interesting enough, in between the selection of firms for the second round and the second presentation, only one of the three firms asked to take an actual complete facilities tour. They had the same outdated blueprints everyone else received, but felt more comfortable seeing the actual facility. While all three presentations were good, the firm that took the time to tour the facilities stood out and eventually won, by identifying the very real challenges we would be facing with this project. All of us on the selection committee had backgrounds with organizations located in more modern facility. We were accustomed to everything in the facilities being consistent – window spacing, all HVAC, power availability, floor access, etc. So needless to say, we were somewhat surprised to hear of the inconsistencies that stood in our way. Although, not insurmountable, time and costs would need to be adjusted to effectively complete this project.

In the above scenario, there were three presentations. The key factor in the presentations was to know what materials you are presenting when and why. In the case of the three finalists, they all had the same direction as to what our goal was we wanted to accomplish with the renovations and they all had the opportunity to tour the facilities and probe for additional information. The winner differentiated themselves by presenting their solution within the confines of the current structure. The other two firms presented how they thought we could or should look at the end of the project without any regard for how the actual structure would interfere with their design. Wonderful ideas, beautifully proposed outcome, wrong building. They basically went into their presentations with blinders on. Their proposals looked like you would take seven floors of the Trump Tower and slide them into the middle of the Empire State building. Both are wonderful structures in their own rite, but their designs cannot be intermingled.

By now, I believe we agree that the essentials to an effective presentation center around knowing your customer well, developing a comprehensive knowledge of their goals, and delivering a proposal that addresses all of their goals – both positive and negative. By negative, I'm referring to the unknowns that would be experienced without a thorough assessment of the situation. As in the example above, one of our goals was to enhance the air conditioning system in our space. However, upon opening the ceiling tiles and seeing the limited space there was available to work with, it was decided to re-balance the air distribution as a more viable and cost-effective solution. Part of a salesperson's responsibilities is to also consult and advise the customer when the opportunity presents itself to improve the situation.

This brings us to the point delivering our presentation. All of the necessary information has been identified – background, goals, what ifs, potential unknowns or customer roadblocks. Now you have assembled all of that information along with your proposed solutions into one tidy presentation. As with any sales call; you begin the presentation thanking the customer in advance for their time, followed by the general benefits statement. As part of a subsequent statement to the opening general benefits statement, you may want to state that your presentation addresses all of your customer's priorities and possibly offers some options to consider. Now would be a good time to inform your audience if or when they can pose questions. Depending on the product or service you are selling and the complexity of the information reviewed during the presentation, it may be wiser to field simple questions during the presentation and defer those questions requiring lengthy or detailed responses until the end. There is no real hard and fast rule regarding this issue. You need to consider mitigating factors such as number of people, level of people, and their impact on the decision making process prior to determining a forum for questions. If in doubt, ask your main contact prior to the presentation if they have a preference or protocol. This scenario comes into play primarily where you are presenting to a larger group of decision makers where attendees may be representing other departments or behaviors not initially involved in the process.

Setting ground rules for presentations may sound like overkill, but I've witnessed well-intentioned interruptions cause sales reps to lose their train of thought and become mired in minutiae, ultimately failing to deliver an important point in the presentation. You've worked hard to get to this stage don't fail at one of the final steps of the decision making process.

Presenting to a group or committee presents a new set of challenges and opportunities. Approach that opportunity just as you would a new prospect call. If possible, gather as much information about the new contacts as possible. Your primary contact should be able to help you with the names and general background information. However, you may continue to pursue other sources such as LinkedIn or Facebook. Attempt to establish as many common points between both organizations and personnel as possible. Common points could include:

- Community Service Initiatives
    - Social – country club memberships, towns of residence, community organizations, religious or political affiliations, etc.
    - Environmental Causes – manufacturing processes – use of recycling, wind or solar power,
    - Social Responsibilities – charitable affiliations
- Key Personnel Backgrounds
    - Education
    - Previous Employers

- Professional Associations
- Corporate Goals / Mission Statement Focus

It's always great to establish common bonds; however, you will need to use them wisely. Common bonds should be used in conjunction with reinforcing the logic of why your companies could work well together as they have a similar focus, goal, or management philosophy. I've heard of and witnessed sales reps misuse commonalities in attempt to become "friends" versus business partners. This approach typically does not work and could discredit your presentation and potential relationship. Always make sure the information you are using is current, credible, and quantifiable. As a buyer, I cannot begin to tell you the number of phone calls alone where the sales rep said our president directed them to call me. All this meant is the rep called our president; spoke with his secretary, who informed them that I was the purchasing contact. As a purchasing agent, I always had fun with these reps. My approach was to attempt to make the rep divulge exactly how he knew our president. Those reps who didn't hang up, usually had to admit this was just a cold call, but that they had a deal that was too good to pass up. It never worked.

So far you have addressed the intangibles – attendees, relationships, personal characteristics, etc. Now it's time to look at the process and set up you will employ to deliver your presentation. First, you'll need to determine what method you will use to deliver your presentation. Again, the answer relies on your audience or customer. Will it be hard copy, PowerPoint, a combination with potential videos, or will it just be spoken with no audio visuals. This truly depends on the product or service you are selling. Since the mid – 90's, for the products and services I sold, PowerPoint was typically the format I employed. There were times I distributed hard copies of testimonials or a system financial analysis, but in general I preferred

PowerPoint. The larger the group; the more information that needs to be delivered, the stronger the need for PowerPoint.

Like anything, PowerPoint can be over-used or misused. My rule of thumb in using PowerPoint is that it delivers discussion points. Do not make the mistake of reading your presentation to your audience. Not only is that rude and insulting, it's boring. I've been on the receiving end of a few of these PowerPoint as well as hard copy presentations and I felt like they were reading me a bed time story. In my mind, the name PowerPoint implies what the presentation format should be used for – a powerful way to deliver your point. If you don't elaborate on the point in your presentation, somebody may get the impression the presentation was put together for you to read. You're in sales, so sell. Show your customer you know your material. Explain the benefit behind the feature or service. You may get feedback that can lead you into identifying additional benefits or reasons why you and your company have the best solution to your customer's needs.

That brings us to an often overlooked concept – the meeting place. Depending on the number of attendees, this is a critical piece you need to know ahead of time. The more intimate the room, the better the chances of connecting with your audience. I've performed presentations in settings ranging from a table in a cafeteria to an auditorium. As long as your audience is able to hear, see, and comprehend your presentation your message should easily be delivered. Sometimes you have the ability to control the setting, sometimes you don't. I've worked for organizations that had one huge conference room. The best way to manage that situation is prepare the room ahead of time, with your contact's approval, so you control where people sit. As an example, if you are presenting to six people in a conference room with twenty chairs, place materials (presentations, hard copies of examples, or just a blank writing pad and pen,) by the chairs where you would like the attendees to sit.

While this may sound elementary, I've witnessed people who like their own space and sit somewhat removed from the other attendees. You always want to make sure that people are part of the presentation process and are engaged with your message. Anyone distancing themselves from the group poses the problem that they may not receive the full benefit of your message. This is equivalent to sitting in the back of the classroom doing homework for the next class that you should have completed the previous evening. There are many sized and shaped rooms; you ultimately want to make sure all the chairs are facing the front of the room or wherever you are delivering your presentation.

The next piece of the presentation you will want to address is the presentation hardware required for effectively delivering your message. If it is as simple as a hard copy presentation or analysis, I would suggest not only providing your copies, but also adding a writing pad for attendees to take notes. Always be prepared for the worst case scenario. As thorough as your presentation may be, there will always be a reason for someone to take additional notes or answers to questions you may not have addressed or clarified. If you don't provide the materials for them to take notes, you may be relegated to relying on a bad memory. Keep in mind, there may be multiple presentations for your product or service. Don't let your message get confused with another vendor's. If you presentation requires use of a laptop with accompanying projector, make sure the equipment is available and working. Even if your prospect or customer confirms they have the projector, bring one from your office in the event their projector isn't available or does not work. Also, make sure you have a spare bulb with you. I wouldn't say that if I didn't witness a sales rep scurrying at the last minute to find a spare bulb. Luckily the facility where the presentation took place had an audio-visual department that had spare bulbs on hand. No bulb, no professional presentation, and you look unprepared. Believe me, this will be the one thing everyone will remember about your presentation, even of you deliver it in hard copy. Although I haven't witnessed a presentation using transparencies for quite some time; the same approach also applies to that equipment as well. Another facet to address is any material handouts, whether it's printed material, samples, sell sheets, or other supporting documents. All materials should be carefully proofread and samples should be tested. Nothing should be left to interpretation that could result in a distraction.

The last piece of preparing for your presentation is doing the test run. Along with testing all of the respective equipment, go through your presentation a few times. You want to sound natural, as though you are just having a conversation. You don't want to sound like a robot delivering a canned message. The purpose of running through your presentation is to make sure you have a complete comfort level with the material. I strongly recommend not memorizing your presentation. One question can disrupt the train of thought and turn a good presentation into one loaded with "uhs and duhs." During this process, also make sure any hard copies of your presentation are in the correct order and there are no materials missing or out of order. Do not provide anyone the perception that you are not thorough or unprepared. Always, always, always have Plan B. I'm not saying bring candles in the event the building loses power, (unless you are a candle sales person,) but always be prepared for anything.

Building confidence in the buyer is vital to a successful presentation. Going back to the interview process, you are aware of the buyer's priorities; you also know their likes and dislikes. Build and deliver your presentation based on their priorities in order of importance. As you did in the interview, get confirmation or buy-in that your proposed solution will satisfy their requirements. Knowing the organization's priorities and delivering solutions shows you have taken the time to understand their requirements and you didn't just deliver a canned presentation of pre-printed sell sheets.

This chapter just identified a few important points of consideration leading up to your presentation. Keep in mind, there is some perceived benefit in the mind of the buyer or you would not have reached this stage. Build on your momentum; keep adding value to the process. Don't ever believe that because you were given the opportunity to deliver a presentation that you have the business locked up. My philosophy is you don't have the business until the invoice is paid and you have confirmed the customer's satisfaction.

Chapter 10

The Presentation – Complete & Competitive

So the table is set and dinner is ready to be served – how will you deliver your presentation? In addition to the topics we reviewed in the previous chapter, do you know enough about the current situation at your prospect to anticipate various situations that could become issues during your presentation? How well do you know the competition in order to fend off situations that may address their strengths? In other words, are you prepared? These are the questions we'll address in this chapter.

Let's begin with determining if your presentation will be extemporaneous or memorized. Depending on you, your comfort level with the materials to be presented, the audience you are presenting to, and the level of details you need to present; there isn't a clear cut answer. My personal approach is an organized version of extemporaneous with a thorough knowledge of my topic. I rehearse a few times or until I have achieved a comfort level with the flow of the presentation. Typically, there are going to be common elements in every presentation you deliver. These are usually your organization's core competencies, which you should be able to recite in your sleep. Extemporaneous presentations in conjunction with PowerPoint or a hard copy presentation are my preferred method. It's my own belief that I sound more natural delivering my presentation this way than using a memorized speech format. I feel that I gain more trust from my audience than trying to deliver the memorized method or constantly reading form note cards, which may give the appearance I don't know or am uncomfortable delivering the information. Extemporaneous presentations also allows for audience interaction. If handled correctly, interaction can lead to additional opportunities. We'll address this later in the chapter.

The key to a successful extemporaneous presentation is to avoid getting too far off track. You will need to know how to control the audience participation to keep the presentation relative to the information you need to deliver and the goal of the presentation. If someone is micro-focused on a bit of non-relevant information; politely say you will gladly address that later or after the presentation and make a note to do so. Know your time limit and be aware of where you are at in the timeframe of your presentation.

Memorizing your presentation is not the worst thing you could do. However, I would highly recommend against it. There are reps who feel more comfortable with memorization. I've had sales reps deliver memorized presentations to me. The first clue was their request to hold all questions until the end of the presentation. The second clue was the fact they sounded like they were reading from cue cards even though I could see they were not. The third clue was they were nervous about losing their place in the presentation. Since I was relegated to holding my questions until the end, I would write down my questions during the presentation. This action apparently made the rep nervous enough because they then had to anticipate what I was going to ask at the end of their presentation. They just came off as unpolished and unprepared. Nervousness has a way making you forget what you were going to say, which in turn makes you more nervous. It's the ultimate catch 22 that you don't want to experience during a presentation. If you do choose to memorize your presentation, the key points to memorize would be:

- The opening or general benefits statement – why are you here and why are they here and how is the next thirty, sixty, or ninety minutes going to improve their life or job.

- The transitions between topics – develop an easy segue between topics, don't sound like you've closed one book and are now opening another, connect the dots for your audience.

- The close – summarize the key points of your message into a concise closing statement. This may be the final time you will be speaking with some of your audience. Make them remember you.

Everybody develops a presentation style they are comfortable with. Go with what works best for you. I've witnessed incredibly slick and professional presentations that ultimately went nowhere for a myriad of reasons. All the toys in the world do not guarantee success. It all comes from you. Put your best foot forward; be tenacious in your follow up, make the prospect / customer your priority and you will succeed more than you fail.

Now we need to appraise the presentation situation. We did a little of this in chapter 9 when we discussed establishing common points. However, when you are appraising the presentation situation, you'll want to know as much detail about everyone involved. It's always good to know if there are loyalties behind the scenes and how well the current source established relationships within the organization. Early in this book we talked about the importance of knowing the likes and dislikes of the prospect's current source. Hopefully by now you've uncovered that information as it relates to your buyer. However, if your competitor also established ties between their organization and your prospect's at various levels, you will have to sell just that much harder. Do your absolute best investigative work to prevent your presentation from being sabotaged by an unknown loyalty factor. All of this comes from your probing skills in your initial interviews and looking into business contacts on social media sites. This is just information that is good to know so you can be prepared for questions related to your competitor or their selling approach and perceived benefits. Knowing this information can easily allow you to anticipate and effectively develop responses to situational strategies. In the twenty first century, vendors are assuming more and more responsibilities in managing their customer's accounts. Just go to the grocery store and watch who is putting products on the shelf. You constantly see employees of the soft drink companies, bread manufacturers, or snack companies stacking the inventory in their displays. The major mass merchants view vendors more favorably if they have an actual employee in their offices managing inventory levels, ordering processes, and other functions related to their product lines versus having someone from the mass merchant's staff performing that task. It's no longer only price that brings success, it's also the other value-added services that can differentiate competitors. Know the complete picture going into your presentation.

In most presentations I've delivered, the topic of the competition has been raised on various levels such as "who is your competition," "why should we switch vendors," "are you aware of who our current vendor is," etc. Be prepared to answer those questions. Obviously, the more you know about your competitor, the easier your responses will flow. However, one thing you should never do is bash the competition. I know from personal experience when being asked a question about certain competitors, in the back of my mind I'm screaming that all they have to offer is price and they'll raise those prices ninety days after you start doing business. However, what I said was that I was aware of them and am quite confident that my proposal and my organization would be a better fit for their company. Don't ever get into specific competitive differences unless your prospect raises a specific issue. Even in that scenario, deliver the message about the benefits of your product or service and confirm how your proposal differs from the competition.

In another situation early on in my sales career, I just finished delivering my presentation to a purchasing committee. Everyone liked what they heard; I had all of the heads nodding in approval for every feature and benefit I proposed in my summary. I finished with the famous "any questions?" I have one said the vice-president who was the lead person on the committee. "Who is your competition?" The first thing that crossed my mind was to name about seven companies off the top of my head, which may have directly answered the question but extended the sales cycle should they have decided to pursue those companies. My response, which even surprised me, was "you can look in the telephone directory for companies that sell the same products as my organization; however, nobody can match our services or customer satisfaction levels." His response was "good answer, let's get started." With that the buyer and I scheduled a meeting to develop the implementation plan and we never looked back.

The bottom line on addressing the competition is do not unless you are asked to. At that time, do it with class and integrity. Don't evade questions about your competitor, but don't give your competitor any ammunition to use against you. If you have never been politically correct, now would be a good time to start. You don't know who in the room knows the competition or may have ties to them. In my purchasing days, I worked for a company where three executives had ties to three different suppliers for the same product. I had to be politically correct as a buyer. The supplier I did select was not tied to any of them; along with the fact this supplier actually showed savings and improved service levels.

Chapter 11

The Presentation – Make It Clear

I cannot stress how important it is to make sure you and your audience are on the same page all through your presentation. Don't assume everyone has the same comprehension level of your product or service as you or your purchasing contact. Keep your presentation interesting for all participants. The best approach to take is the use of effective visuals. By this, I mean visuals that support the point(s) you are trying to deliver to your audience.

In chapter ten we reviewed the positives and negatives of using PowerPoint. In reality, whatever presentation method you employ, to be successful you will need to confirm your point is understood by all. If you are using visuals, make sure they are easily understood. Try not to have too many moving pieces of information displayed at one time where you will have the audience's eyes roaming all over the slide. If you are trying to make a point and are required to use visuals that resemble the Los Angeles freeway system; have a legend somewhere on the page that allows the audience to understand your point. Walk them through your visual and as you are explaining the details, watch the facial expressions and general body language. If you see anyone who appears confused, uncomfortable, or generally disinterested; ask if there are any questions. Without singling out the individual, try to get their feedback on the information before moving on to the next topic. Maybe preface your question with, "I know there is a lot of information on one page, but this directly relates to *(whatever the topic may be)* and the importance to your organization is….. Always try to picture how the person is going to interpret your material once they are no longer in your presentation. You do not want anyone to draw their own conclusions. Especially when addressing key points or the customer's priorities, confirm that everyone understands and comprehends the point you are trying to deliver. That being said, make sure your presentation has some life to it. This is a balancing act between what you like and the culture of your customer. This is one of the key reasons it is important to know your customer. If you are presenting to an accounting firm where everyone wears dark suits, white shirts or blouses, and a red tie; format your presentation in a conservative design. If delivering your presentation in PowerPoint, use little or no animations. Be clear, concise, and to the point. Remember in the finance world, black is good, red is bad. Conversely, if you are presenting to an advertising agency where you are working with creative folks, the use of color and animations are more acceptable. However, don't go over the top and try to make a home movie out of your presentation. A simple rule of thumb is to ask the question, "Does this visual make my presentation clearer?"

A classic example of this happened to me when my largest account was comparing us with my primary competitor. I had a great relationship with this account over the course of nine years. However, their new vice president of finance was having all vendors reviewed for additional cost savings. It would have been very easy for me to say, "take another five or ten percent and we'll call it a day." This was not the approach to take for a number of reasons. We'll address those reasons in chapters twelve and thirteen.

My approach was to have the customer visit our facilities for a product and service review. The goal was to propose alternate products that would save them money and at the same time increase my company's profits. We also wanted to discuss operational and account management changes that would improve their overall procurement and delivery systems. This entailed incorporating their purchasing volume on a national basis versus locally as had been done in the past. I could have easily compiled an Excel spreadsheet that showed product numbers, costs, usage, savings, etc. However, since this comparison entailed over 125 products, I wanted to make an impact. It would be very easy to show a bottom line of projected savings, but I wanted to make those savings scream "CHOOSE ME" at the customer. To do this, I took a sample of every current item that was on their high usage list. I labeled each item with their current local annual volume, current national volume based on reports supplied by the customer, purchase price, and total annual expenditures. I then took a sample of alternate or generic products. These were items that were either from another manufacturer or the current manufacturer's private label brand. These items were in either different packaging or maybe a slightly different color. There was absolutely no difference in quality or function of the product. I then labeled these items using the same data as above, but showed the savings represented by changing to the alternate product. All of these items were then placed on our long conference table in the order of product category. At the end of the table was a covered picture frame on an easel. When the buyer and his manager arrived and were escorted into the conference room, much to their surprise, they were greeted by this vast array of product. After facilitating a brief meeting with our vice president and national accounts coordinator to define and confirm my customer's expectations; we reviewed each product so they could get a picture of the minimal changes they would need to make to obtain their potential savings. At the end of the product review, I unveiled the picture that showed a picture of a check made out to my customer in the amount of the projected annual savings, which were quite substantial. At the end of the review, I asked the all-important question, "Are there any questions?" To which they laughed and said, "Let's sit down and map out the next steps." At that stage, we sat down to dot the *i's,* cross the *t's,* and schedule a time to develop an implementation plan.

The point in all of this was that I knew my customer and I knew my competitor. My customer is visual and I knew they wanted to see savings. We displayed their savings in living color and not only in a spreadsheet. We also developed a map showing their regional offices they wanted to include in the program along with our local distribution centers that would service those locations. My competitor, on the other hand, would provide them with a revised price list with a couple of product suggestions and a list of their distribution centers. We came away after the first year with $1.6 million in business and increased our gross profit margin by eleven points. This was certainly well worth the effort.

As I've stated many times, know your customer and know your audience. Also, a small detail, but when using your computer to deliver your presentation, be cognizant of the wallpaper you have showing when you start your computer along with the screen savers you display as your computer is idle at the end of your presentation. Change your settings to eliminate what could be perceived by the customer as controversial material – political, religious, personal choice of music, hobbies, etc. If you have to think about whether material is acceptable or not; do not display it. Make sure the volume on your cellphone is off as well as the notifications sound on your computer. Again, you have worked so hard to get to this point; don't let some unrelated business issue detract from you and your organization's image.

Chapter 12

Handling Objections

An objection is simply a statement related to a person's understanding that your product or service will not completely satisfy their requirements. In one regard, an objection is a good sign that the buyer is processing the information you are delivering. Early in my sales career, I interviewed a buyer and walked through all of the stages of the products and services we provided along with addressing all of their requirements. Delivered the presentation a week later and again walked through the entire process of what happens when an order is placed along with how and when they can expect delivery. As I relayed in previous chapters, I confirmed the buyer's understanding of each feature and moved on to the next. She placed a nice order and the supplied were delivered as promised the next day. The day after I called to confirm everything was as she expected and to my surprise, she went ballistic. The buyer wanted multiple delivery points within the building, did not like the shelving units she ordered, and said she could not accept backorders. I offered to meet with her that afternoon and address her issues. We reviewed each issue and I was able to clarify and solve the misunderstandings. I brought my notes from the interview and presentation to show her what we agreed to, but at the same time said we would deliver everything in accordance with her demands. However, this lady was so upset, her resolution was to personally attack the credibility of me and my company. Even though she agreed she was not clear about her requirements and didn't understand the difference between a backorder and a special custom order, she wanted to take the easy way out and remain with her current source. Later on I found out that this lady did not have the authority to make the change in suppliers, along with the fact their current supplier was a relative of the president. That experience taught me to be a little more cautious of prospect's that have no objections to anything.

One example of an objection could be where a company is looking for a specific format of invoicing for your products or services and your systems group cannot deliver that solution. Another example is your equipment can process 250 widgets per minute and the customer's requirement is 450. My view of an objection is that it is really an opportunity. Unless there is some inherent logical reason an objection cannot be overcome, I would use it as an opportunity to continue the sales process.

Never walk away from an objection. You may know you can't completely satisfy the customer's objection, but at least show them that you and your organization are willing to address their needs. Advise your customer you believe you can satisfy their request, but need to confirm with the proper personnel. Never commit to something you cannot deliver. If it is an issue you can resolve on the spot and you are authorized to approve the solution, do it. It shows the customer you have authority to address issues and gives them confidence your company trusts your judgment. The worst thing is for a sales rep to constantly say they need to get it approved. It just adds one more delay to the sales process and customer satisfaction. Every organization has their limits of authority afforded to sales reps. Most everybody I know has had the experience of the car sales person who had to constantly go check with their manager to see if they could lower the price, include an option, or waive a fee. Talk about frustrating – don't be that person.

When addressing an objection, the first rule is to confirm that you completely comprehend the customer's point of view. Depending on the complexity, you may want to analyze the objection in stages. A simple objection is "your price is too high." A more complex objection could be related to a situation where multiple departments are affected by the proposed solution. It is extremely important not only to your success, but to the customer's impression of you, that you comprehend and deliver a solution that addresses their needs.

Sometimes the solution may be a compromise or an opportunity to close the sale; "if I can deliver this system in complete compliance with your requests, can we close the deal today?" This will either close the deal or lead to additional objections, but you will certainly know where you stand.

When should you address an objection? In most cases, immediately. The only exceptions are if the objection relates to a solution you know you are going to discuss later in the conversation or if you are in the middle of a presentation and the response to the issue would interrupt the flow or content. This would be a scenario you need to have a feeling for, depending on who is presenting the objection, as well as the importance of the objection. If it's a deal breaker, the objection needs to be addressed immediately or no matter how well the balance of your presentation is delivered, the net result will be no sale. An incident occurred when I was in purchasing and it was related to an equipment maintenance agreement we had with a local office equipment repair organization. We were experiencing longer than agreed to response times, improper repairs requiring multiple visits to resolve one issue, and replacement parts that ultimately were not required, but were invoiced. If it were just a couple of delays or mistakes, I would understand, but it was becoming the norm. I scheduled a meeting with the vendor to address these issues and come to a resolution moving forward. The vendor brought along his new service manager who was there to sell me on revised procedures they were implementing, which all sounded fine. However, they thought that everything from the past would just be swept under the rug and this was day one of our "new" relationship. However, my goal was two-fold; reimburse my company for the documented billing errors as well as a pro-rated amount of the agreement that they did not fulfill. This is an example of an objection that you should address immediately. The owner of the company informed me that he would review the billing errors and let me know if he thought we were due a refund, which was mistake number one as I felt that he didn't trust the information I was providing. His second mistake was saying he didn't feel there was any reason to issue a refund for not living up to the service levels established in the agreement. That by hiring a new service manager, he was correcting that issue and we should be moving forward. With the obvious disparity in our expectation levels, I declared the meeting over and immediately wrote the contract cancellation letter as specified in our agreement. We eventually did receive a refund for the billing errors as this was a documented fraudulent business practice. Our new service provider performed in a stellar fashion.

Addressing an objection also shows the decision makers how well prepared you are to consider other options or approaches for solutions to their issues. Preparing for objections begins with concepts we talked about in earlier chapters – thoroughly know your prospect's needs and likes, know your competitor's capabilities and weaknesses, and know your capabilities. Knowing your competitor's capabilities and weaknesses is a constant moving target that can easily change from day to day. The competitor's sales reps can also have an impact as they could be either one of the strengths or weakness, depending on their customer relationship skills. As a manager, I put together a reference resource on our top competitors. The information included their top accounts, sales rep's profiles, strengths and weaknesses, and key account strategies. This was no different than a football coach studying film on the next opponent. The more information you have, the better you can react, and the more success you will realize.

Now for the most difficult objection – the hidden or false objection. The underlying reason typically has little or nothing to do with your actual capabilities, but more to do with a relationship with the current vendor's company or sales rep. Let's take the example from chapter 8 regarding the widget manufacturer. As it related to special orders, the current manufacturer requires a 50% down payment and a long lead time. Your solution was to schedule the production runs for the seasonal widgets and store them for the customer thus reducing the long lead time and eliminating the down payment. As long as your price is competitive, it sounds like a no-brainer for the buyer to convert the business to you. However, you could be surprised by a rejection. Further probing could unveil a hidden objection such as this manufacturer assisted the supplier in securing business for their products, or the manufacturer may have extended favorable payment terms during a difficult financial time for the supplier.

Another example of a hidden objection is delivered in chapter 6, where we had every logical business reason to relocate our clerical operation. We documented all of the hard and soft cost savings. We didn't relocate as a result of the president affection for the local area.

How do you uncover those hidden objections? Additional probing and trial closes. At this stage you have presented all facets of your product and services to your client. They have been in complete agreement that you capabilities meet their needs. At this stage all you can do is review the presentation and gain confirmation from the prospect that each feature and benefit meets or exceeds their requirements and finally ask the question, "what is it you need that I am not delivering?" In most cases, if you receive an honest answer, it will have nothing to do with capabilities, but will usually relate to a business relationship at a higher level within the company. You may also ask, "Now that I've showed you the way the issue of ……., is there anything that would come in the way of converting the business to my organization?" Personally, I've been on both sides of this situation. I've had customers who wouldn't even take a call from a competitor because they didn't believe anyone could come close to providing the attention and service I gave to my customers. On the other hand, I've lost an opportunity or two because my competitor had that same level of relationship within their accounts. At that stage, my response was to always keep me in mind should their current source not be able to satisfy their requirements or if a special need should arise that would require immediate attention.

On the other hand a false objection is just a fictitious reason for the buyer to either gain the upper hand in negotiations or eliminate you from consideration in moving forward with your proposal.

A typical false objection is "your price is too high." Again, the way to address this is with open and closed probes. If you are supplying one price as in say a construction project, you may want to review each facet to confirm you have the correct understanding and properly addressed the respective specifications. In chapter 10, I relayed a situation of an old building I worked which was located in downtown Chicago. One of the construction projects related to an entire floor which was bid out for total renovation. The architect put together all of the contractor specifications related to every facet of the construction project. The bid was issued to six contractors who had experience with older facilities in and around our location. From previous bids, we knew all of the contractors should be within 10% of each other. To our surprise, one company came in close to 25% under the next lowest bid. Sounds wonderful – right? Time to review the bid to make sure he is providing the materials we specified. We discovered hollow core doors where solid core was specified, altered electrical specs, subpar window treatments, and a list of other little changes the contractor made without providing those in writing. In this example, the very real objection was, "your price is too low." However, my point is to make sure you review every aspect of your proposal with your prospect to make sure they understand your submission. We also went through the same exercise with the highest bidder because I felt in my initial interview with them they had the best comprehension and responses to our unique building situation.

This is also a great opportunity to gather information on how the competition is responding and pricing the respective products or services. Consequently, if you are just dismissed from the process without being afforded the opportunity to review your proposal with the buyer, you probably didn't have a chance to secure the business in the first place. There are buyers who just audit their current supplier by checking prices in the market place. Some have absolutely no intention of changing sources, but are merely using the competitor's sales reps as a measuring stick. It would be nice to have a crystal ball or a litmus test you could administer to a buyer to see if the opportunity is authentic. Early in my sales career I received a bid from a large insurance company. If I win this opportunity, I am one of the big hitters in my first year. I went to discuss the opportunity with one of the sales managers. He suggested I have a pre-bid meeting with the buyer and determine at what level of price savings would I need provide in order to take the business away from the incumbent. The buyer was reluctant to schedule a meeting, but eventually did meet with me. She was very non-committal about everything – services, pricing, representation expectations. I returned from the meeting and immediately met with the sales manager. He just laughed and said the rep currently servicing the account was a former employee of our company and took that business with him when he left. He knew the rep and the buyer had a great relationship and there was no way she was going to change back to us. I respectfully returned the bid with a letter explaining that while we were flattered to receive the opportunity, we didn't feel we had enough to offer her and her organization in the way of price or process improvements that would provide enough reasons to convert their business. Obviously, I struck a nerve because I received a scathing voice mail stating we would never again get the opportunity to bid on their business. Reading between the lines, she had to go to another vendor to be the audit point and she didn't receive our information to pass along to her current supplier.

Chapter 13

The Close

A successful close is like a walk-off homer in baseball or a "Hail-Mary" touchdown pass to win the football game. This is the situation where you are taking everything you've learned about your prospect and responding with your solutions to get that agreement to move forward with them. We've talked about trial closes with the "If I / would you?" questions, which are great if what you are proposing at the time is a deal breaker that secures the business. It's always great when you can cut to the chase. The sooner you start selling, the sooner you begin making money and improving your customers business. However, most sales processes will follow a pattern you have read about up to this point. The close is the final piece of the sales process puzzle in securing the business.

There are a multitude of philosophies on closing and I'm sure most, if not all, are accurate. However, for an effective close, you need the following:

- A thorough knowledge of the prospects overall needs, wants, and priorities.

- The solution to effectively address those needs, wants, and priorities.

- A closing statement that takes all of the features and benefits of your product or services the buyer has agreed with you that would be an improvement to their organization.

- An effective delivery that is concise, but yet leaves room for the buyer to add their comments along the way. A buyer never wants to feel like they are trapped into buying something.

- Lastly, the courage to deliver that closing statement.

Let's review these steps in depth:

- A thorough knowledge of the prospects overall needs, wants, and priorities – you probably would not get the opportunity to close if you didn't have this knowledge. That's not to say you may not uncover a hidden need in the closing process. This is especially true as it relates to multiple decision makers involved in the final decision. Should a hidden need arise, you should be able to address it on the spot. By now the prospect's priorities should have been identified.

- The solution to effectively address those needs, wants, and priorities – this is where your knowledge of your organization's capabilities comes into play. Know exactly what you are going to propose, along with having a backup plan in place. Anticipate, and I cannot stress this strongly enough, the responses you may receive to your closing statement. By not having a definite response to a solution, you have just kept the door open for your competition. The last thing you want to do at this stage is delay their decision.

- A closing statement that takes all of the features and benefits of your product or services the buyer has agreed with you that would be an improvement to their organization – present this in a manner that you feel the prospect would be comfortable with. I could develop a list of "not to do's," but there are some buyers who are comfortable with various closing styles. Personally, I never wanted to sound like a trial lawyer delivering the closing arguments, but there are some buyers who like that style. Deliver the features and benefits in your closing statement in line with how the buyer prioritized them. Again, get their buy in on each item, and then deliver your closing statement.

- An effective delivery that is concise, but yet leaves room for the buyer to add their comments along the way. A buyer never wants to feel like they are trapped into buying something – "Mr. or Mrs. Buyer, we've reviewed you and your organization's priorities in converting your business to my organization. Let's review your priorities and our proposed solutions, make sure we've addressed all of your priorities, and review or develop a plan to move forward. Does that sound okay to you?" In essence, that is a trial close on its own. Unless you are completely out of touch with the process, the buyer will agree to continue the conversation. Depending on the situation of when you are closing the account will depend on how you proceed with your closing statement. If you are closing at the end of a presentation, you may summarize your features and benefits and use that as part of your closing statement, with the question – "If you agree that our proposal would address or improve, *(fill in the blank)* can we proceed with the implementation plan? At this stage, there is only one thing for you to do as Tom Hopkins clearly states in his training materials – SHUT UP! Do not backtrack, do not hem and haw and say, "Oh well I mean......." You are closing; it's yes or no, a hit or a foul ball, I do or I might. This is where the buyer either commits or says they need more information or changes in the proposal. That one little question will tell you exactly where you stand with your prospect.

- Lastly, the courage to deliver that closing statement – I've witnessed good sales reps crumble when it comes to closing the sale. Close the sale with casual confidence. The buyer must be interested to some level or you wouldn't have gotten this far in the sales process. Do not change your manner when you start to proceed with your closing statement. Speak warmly; don't change your tone, voice inflection, or pace at which you speak. Don't rush through the closing process or you may arouse suspicions in your buyer that you are trying to push them into a decision.

We've addressed different methods and techniques. Now let's review timing. The best time to close is when you begin to receive buying signs. What is a buying sign? The typical buying sign can occur at any time during your initial interview, follow up conversations, presentation, or subsequent reviews. I've closed accounts based on the strength of a letter, while it took multiple meetings to advance the sales process with others. A buying sign can be communicated verbally such as asking additional questions about your product, agreeing with your statements, or discussing opportunities that would occur if they owned your product. A buying sign can also be communicated visually such as a buyer smiling when you discuss or demonstrate the product or request to see additional features of the product. All of these are buying signs.

The key to delivering a trial close is to know the importance of the feature and benefit to the buyer and their organization. Never assume the feature and benefit value is the same for all buyers. The quickest way to determine the value is to first confirm the buyer understands the feature and benefit, then ask the question, "How important is that feature and benefit to you and your organization?" If the buyer responds that it is critical to their operation, go for the close – "If I can deliver this product in two days or one week, could we place the order today?" The best case is you get the order; the worst case is you get a "no," but still are able to continue with the presentation / demonstration. If the buyer responds that the feature is something that is important, but not critical, continue on with your presentation. Now is not the time for a trial close. Every sales scenario is different. I'm not sure if I would use a trial close on the first buying sign I received on the first feature, but again it all depends on your relationship with the buyer and the product or service you are selling.

The company I work for manufactures and sells consumable products to independent retail stores. As part of the sales process, whenever a sales rep visits a new store, I have them set up the store in our on-line ordering system prior to the visit. As part of the demonstration, the rep will pull up their account in the system on the store's computer and offer to place an order right there for them, with a suggestion of testing the top five selling products. At that time the rep will also add our ordering site to their Shortcuts or Favorites on their computer. This of course is done after the product demonstrations and getting the buyer's approval to consider adding our products to their store. It also shows the buyer how easy it is to order on-line. Two sales approaches are accomplished here for the positive. The first is we have everything pre-set in our system; we don't resort to fumbling around with order forms or account set up forms. The transition from the buying sign to the actual purchase is fairly seamless. The second is the reps are able to see the sales from the buyer's perspective. They can see which products the store currently sells and why the buyer would carry those products. They can then proceed to sell the idea our products will enhance the store's sales as a result of our high quality, unique features, and great reputation.

Another sales tool for closing is to offer a tour of your facilities, depending on logistics. Keep in mind a facilities tour is also a sales tool. A tour should be used to reinforce the features and benefits you have reviewed with your prospect to this stage. Of course, you need to know how your facilities measure up to that of your competitors, but a picture speaks a thousand words. For a prospect to see your processes in action, whether it's manufacturing, distribution, or service center functions, could finalize their decision and close the sale faster than phone calls and follow up meetings. The key component of a facilities tour is you and your sales ability. Too often I've witnessed reps who view a tour as a day to walk around and show off your prospect to other employees and grab a free lunch. Just because you are not at your prospect's office doesn't mean you don't need to keep selling. A facilities tour is a prime opportunity to differentiate you from the competition. Know your prospect's needs and wants and make sure they see exactly how you can meet and hopefully, exceed their expectations.

A tour is just like a human PowerPoint presentation. When I brought prospects in for a tour, I made sure that each department I visited knew the prospect was coming out that day and was aware of any specific topic that related to the prospect's priorities that would be affected by their department. As an example, one of my prospects needed resources to follow up on any item we did not typically carry in our inventory. When we toured the Purchasing Department, the supervisor raised this issue and described the system in place to address the prospect's needs. We all confirmed that our system would work for the prospect before moving on. A similar conversation occurred when we toured the warehouse and reviewed the ability to stock the prospect's special needs to reduce the delivery time. Again, everyone confirmed that this was acceptable. The best approach is to make your prospect feel comfortable and part of the process and/or solution. When the prospect hears the same message from your internal personnel, it will lend credibility to your sales process. Most importantly, prior to leaving one department for another, confirm their needs have been met and that all of their questions have been answered.

Before ending the tour, confirm that they do not have any further questions and that they have seen everything they needed to see to make a decision. If the timing is right, use a trial close by starting to review a summary of your implementation plan. Say something like, "If everything you've seen today meets your expectations, here's the next step we should move towards." Gauge the feedback you receive from the prospect. If there is no hesitation to the implementation plan, schedule a time to meet and confirm the times for the implementation activities. Ideally, finalize the plan at the end of the tour. Do not leave any stone unturned.

Lastly, if your other trial close was met by hesitation, ask the question, "Given everything you've seen today, is there any reason you would not move forward with our proposal?" Assuming the tour went well, the setting is perfect for a trial close. If you don't attempt a trial close at this stage, you have just wasted a lot of time and money.

So if closing is just a combination of knowledge, effective communication, and timing, why is it so tough for sales reps to close? I've worked with numerous reps over the years and there isn't any one magical answer, except for lack of confidence. Age, sex, race, hair color, or shoe size have nothing to do with a rep's closing skills. I've worked with reps who have excellent sales skills; they can uncover prospects and network like a politician. However, when it comes to sealing the deal, they fall apart like a crumb cake. They lacked the confidence in having the buyer give their effort the stamp of approval. In other words, they were comfortable talking about the buyer's needs and priorities and selling their capabilities to the prospect, but when it came time to ask the "If I / would you" question, they couldn't pull the trigger. Some reps felt they didn't have overwhelming benefits to offer, others just had a fear of rejection and never having the opportunity to come back, while others said they couldn't deal with the pressure at that time.

In my sales experience, I felt the toughest part of the sale was getting that first appointment. Once I got my foot in the door, I was confident we would be doing business. I couldn't get to the closing process soon enough. My confidence level in closing new business was the result of doing my homework and knowing my organization offered the best solution to the prospect's requirements.

The next couple of pages contain outline versions of the closing process.

Closing

"People love to buy after they own."

Buyers only have a problem with indecision, insecurity, and procrastination before they own. The skilled sales rep makes buyers feel like they already own it. - Tom Hopkins

1. **Educate & sell with enthusiasm**
   - **Retailers wanted to buy direct, now they can.**
   - **Reinforce how easy it is to order online.**
   - **Reinforce the control they have as a retailer who is set up in our system.**
     - Place orders
     - Check on order status
     - Change orders prior to shipment
     - Print confirmations and invoices
2. **Close the sale through your buyer's eyes**
   - **See features & benefits of products and services from the buyer's viewpoint**
   - **Weigh features and benefits on their scale**
   - **Close on the benefits that are of value to the customer**
     - Product selection
     - One-stop shopping

- Delivery
- On line access
- Minimum order level

3. When do you close the sale?
    - When the buyer slows down or speeds up the pace of the sale.
    - When they've been listening, but suddenly start asking lots of questions.
    - When they give you positive stimulus at the right time. Questions on:
        - Delivery
        - Pricing
        - Minimum orders
    - When they say "yes" to your test close.
    - Know your customer - Some can't handle the idea of completing online forms.

4. Where do you close?
    - Ideally, in the store during your visit.
    - Via the phone / e-mail
        - Initial Order - already have store set up in the system.
        - Know their product preferences
        - Know their current product selection (ours & competitors)
        - Propose minimum order and be prepared to add items you know they carry from competitors.

The Anatomy of the Close

1. **Understand Your Buyer's Needs & Wants**
   a. **Qualify them thoroughly**
      i. **Emotional Wants**
         1. Save time
         2. Better service
         3. Product selection
      ii. **Financial Stability**
   b. **Understand the buyer's motives**
      i. **Know their likes & dislikes**
         1. Products
         2. Services
      ii. **Determine logic behind likes & dislikes**
         1. Experience with other products
         2. Experience with other company
2. **Recognize Buying Signs**
   a. **Verbal**
      i. Ask additional questions
      ii. Agree with your statements
      iii. Develop a need for more information
      iv. Talk about opportunities that would occur if they owned our products
   b. **Visual**
      i. The buyer's smile
      ii. Ask to see the product or additional techniques demonstrated
      iii. Ask to review product / service features and benefits
3. **Make The Decision**
   a. Communicate that the best thing to do is buy the products and offer it to their customers.
   b. Reinforce the decision to buy based on what you know about their likes and what they feel is important.
4. **Close the Sales with Casual Confidence**
   a. Get to the order screen and start entering or writing the order

      b. If the customer stops you, revisit and address any concerns they have
5. Don't Change When You Start Closing
      a. Speak warmly
           i. Ordering System - "This is very simple, here's all we need to do...."
           ii. Products – "Your customers are going to love the new refillable dispensers and how easy they are to customize and refill."
      b. Don't change your tone, manner, or pace at which you speak.
      c. Don't rush through the ordering process.

The 14 Most Important Words in the Art of Closing

"Whenever You Ask The Closing Question, SHUT UP. The First Person To Speak Loses."

- Tom Hopkins

Chapter 14

Departure & Follow Up

There is not a better feeling in your sales career than closing a sale after you've put in the necessary effort with the prospective buyer. Just having that moment of satisfaction when the buyer reaches across the table to shake your hand and say, "let's get the order or process started," justifies all of your hard work and time spent qualifying their needs and wants. Depending on the size of the account and the amount of work you put into the process, it's hard not to do an end zone celebration dance. However, you still need to act professional and give the buyer the impression that this is not something out of the ordinary for you or your company. The best way to handle your success is to merely thank the buyer and proceed to the implementation or ordering process. This may be as simple as taking the order at that time or scheduling another meeting to review various steps required to implement your program.

Personally, I never felt like I closed the deal until the customer was satisfied with the merchandise and/or service. Just because you closed the sale, don't go into comfort mode and think the work is over. Depending on your company's offering, you always want additional sales or to penetrate the account for additional product placement. In short, you need to keep proving yourself every minute of every day. Always bring value to the relationship.

Okay, you've sealed the deal. You are a hero within your organization. Get those pats on the back all the way down the hallway. Sit down, put your feet up, take a deep breath, and manage a huge smile. Okay, celebration is over. Now everyone or every department within your company who could potentially interface with the new client needs to know when they will commence buying from you and all of the necessary services they will need to provide. Ideally, you can match up respective personnel from your company to the client's organization. This could be having your accounts receivable person contact someone in your clients accounts payables department to introduce themselves and provide contact information should there be any questions or concerns. Should there be multiple departments involved, it might be wise to assemble a respective personnel directory you and your purchasing contact could manage.

Now, for the flip side of the coin, you didn't seal the deal. Now what do you do? In my purchasing days, I've delivered the no sale message to a number of sales reps. Reactions from the reps varied; some asked great questions regarding my choice of the competition, while others just shrugged and left, never to be heard from again. Some reps followed up occasionally with hopes of future opportunities, which is a behavior that can only help build the relationship. As long as you have the relationship; why just walk away and have to start from the beginning a year or two later. It's easier to nurture the relationship than begin the prospecting process all over again. What I found to be strange were the companies who never followed up with me. Not only did the reps never call back, but their companies never assigned another rep to my account for any potential opportunities. Win or lose, follow up is extremely vital to the success or potential development of the relationship. No doesn't mean no forever.

My no sale strategy was as follows:

1. Schedule a meeting or a conference call with the buyer with the purpose of getting to identify why you did not secure the business.

2. As with the closing statement, ask why, then SHUT UP! Don't give the buyer a list of reasons to choose from. Let them tell you in their own words why the opportunity was given to the competitor.

3. After you hear their reasoning you may want to confirm that you did meet all of their expectations so you know for your own benefit that you did all that you could do, just somebody else did it better. You may also uncover new information about the prospect or the competitor, which is always beneficial for future reference. I have an interesting story I'll share later in this chapter regarding this point.

4. Depending on your product or service, uncover when the next opportunity will arise. Make note of it and establish a follow up timetable for yourself.

5. Offer to serve as a backup source or resource for their needs. This is also another way of allowing yourself back in the door to keep the relationship moving forward.

6. If you know your competitor's weakness and you believe it could impact the prospect, check in every so often to measure the prospect's satisfaction level with the current program. Some buyers need to get to a comfort level with a new company and sales rep. As long as they are open to future contact, take advantage of the situation and develop the relationship. At this stage you have nothing to lose.

You obviously do not want to get in the habit of implementing the no sale strategy, but be prepared in the event your efforts result in no sale.

Back to my no sale strategy, point three. My largest account, which was now being managed by another sales rep since I was promoted to management, decided to convert to the competitor. I assisted the current rep with preparing the bid response and was surprised to hear that we did not secure an extended agreement. Having had a long term relationship with the buyer, I requested a "no sale" exit strategy meeting to determine exactly why we didn't achieve the favorable response. I knew that overall it wasn't just related to price; the competitor also had another division of their corporation that was a paper company. This account had over 2,000 employees in the Chicagoland area who used an inordinate amount of paper. The competitor offered a great price on the paper as well as the day-to-day supplies. My company did not have that luxury of including that commodity. That was one of the major differences. They pointed out some other price comparisons that on higher ticket items that just did not make any sense. Knowing my competitor as well as the sales rep who responded to this bid, I was well aware the customer was not going to receive the products they identified in their bid. I prefaced my response in a soft non-threatening way, but drove home my point with a bulldozer. My response related to the fact that the ten higher priced items were being sold to them at or below cost. I also knew these were not stock items for my competitor so there was no way they were going to receive the products they specified in their bid. I advised the buyer to watch those items closely as to when they were ordered and what they received. Also, I knew there was an industry-wide price increase on paper in the next sixty days, and made the buyer aware to check the invoices they received from the new supplier. This is why it is important to know your competition. Of the ten higher priced items, none were received as specified. Even though product and manufacturer numbers were supplied in the bid documents, the items received did not meet the specifications. Also the price increase on the paper was passed along to this account. Within the agreement, the buyer clearly stated any paper price increases would require a written ninety day advance notice. My company had our business back in four months and the competition was out the door.

In another scenario, going against the same competitor on a piece of business neither of us were supplying, the final decision came down to our two companies. This was a difficult bid to respond to as it was loaded with a list of their highly used daily supplies totaling around five hundred, but also performance clauses with penalties for backorders and/or service issues; along with resource requirements to supply dedicated staff to managing their account on top of annual volume rebates and allowances. Developing a response to this bid was similar to assembling a two thousand piece jigsaw puzzle. The fact we were chosen as one of the two finalists told me we did something right, but now for the moment of truth. Our competitor was awarded the business. In the "no sale" strategy meeting it was uncovered that we did everything they required and could easily service their account. As it related to price, there was little or no difference. However, in the end, the competitor estimated the volume of what this contract would represent in sales dollars and gave the customer their volume rebate upfront. Note to self – here's a new ace in the hole. Kudos to my competitor for their forward thinking and taking the $25,000 risk.

Whether you win or lose the business, follow up is tantamount to your potential success. You certainly need to follow up with a customer for a myriad of reasons if you want to keep, maintain, and grow their business. However, following up with an account where you lost the business is just as important. By following up, you are exhibiting the fact that you still care and want to earn their business. It's also keeping the proverbial foot in the door should there be organizational changes. I would entertain that most successful sales reps could share a story of the phone call they received from the "new" buyer inviting them in for a review of their products and services as a result of a follow up call or something that was on file with their contact info. I know I've had my quota of calls that fit that mold. At one point I had three in one month that resulted in over $50,000 in furniture sales. These were the result of follow up with the former buyer who had my information on file. When the buyer left the organization, my information was on file that my company also had a contract furniture division. One of the first projects for the new buyer was to replace the furniture in one of the service departments. As luck would have it, the buyer pulled my information from the file and gave me a call. As one of my managers once said, "hard work creates luck." My "hard work" in this instance was just providing a quarterly follow up information packet regarding the various services my company provided. Eventually, through excellent service and competitive pricing, I did earn the majority of their business. I cannot stress the importance of follow up. In my mind, I never lost an account, they just delayed saying yes to me.

How do you follow up? Periodically communicate with your contacts within the prospect's organization. Let your contacts know that you still have their best interests in mind; a new buyer or process change could open the door for you. In this hi tech age and all of the information that is available on the internet, there are numerous ways to follow up. As an example, LinkedIn provides the capability to follow a company. This information will provide you with personnel, personnel changes, and news regarding the company's business. Revisit the information in chapter 7 that reviews prospecting activities. There are also multiple resources for information about your prospective client that are current and readily available. Effectively manage the process of gathering that data. Make it a point to schedule a time when you research your list of prospects to uncover any information that may lead to an opportunity for immediate follow up. Don't wait for it to appear in a business journal. By the time it appears in print, you've lost two or three months. Also, keep your prospect informed of changes to your product or service offering. When doing so, keep in mind, you want to personalize the message with the "what's in it for me." In other words, what does this new product or service mean to your prospect? How is it going to make their life better? Will it save them time, money, or both? When I was in purchasing, too often I would receive a brochure with a business card stapled to it and a hand written note of "call me if you're interested." Talk about a waste of time and postage. That effort does not constitute follow up. Hopefully, you will provide enough information that will lead to further communication between you and the prospect. You want your communication piece, be it a brochure, e-mail, or sample to be meaningful and have an impact.

Enough on the topic of steps to take when you've lost the business; let's get back to our winning ways. You've won; you've had your celebratory period, now let's get working on activities to cement that relationship.

Step 1 – Confirm everything you and your new client agreed to. Leave absolutely no room for the "I thought you said or I thought you meant." Surprises are great for birthday parties, but horrible for business relationships. Depending on your product or service, you may want to assemble a team from your company and your client's to review product or service specifications. Again, it depends on the complexity of the product or project.

Step 2 – By now, you should have confirmed all of the pricing, product/project specifications as well as service requirements – invoice timing and formats, management reports, special delivery requirements and any other nuances associated with this effort. As mentioned earlier in the chapter, establish a line of communication between your two organizations. As an example, for major accounts, I always had someone from our accounting department contact the customer's accounts payables person to confirm invoice formats, terms and conditions, and to make sure they understood the working relationship. We would also discuss any special requirements with the receiving personnel to make sure we were aware of any special requirements, such as delivery trucks, pallet sizes, and hours of operation. Confirm that everyone involved is aware of the proper person or department to contact to obtain relative information, whether it's questions related to invoicing, deliveries, next step of the project, etc. Always, always, always, make sure everyone knows they can contact you if needed. It's okay to delegate some customer contact if it will get the customer taken care of in a more expedient manner. However, make sure everyone knows they can come to you at any time.

Step 3 – Establish a reasonable time to review the satisfaction level from both the client as well as your company. Depending on the relationship, my recommendation would be no longer than 90 days should transpire before the first complete review. After the first review, I would recommend quarterly or semi-annual reviews. These reviews should focus on the key elements of the business relationship as well as address potential opportunities. Reviews should be presented in a way that they contain measurable information such as order fill, line fill, on-time deliveries, cost containment, or any measurable statistic that relates to your business relationship. Identify the areas where everyone met their targets as well as those that need improvement. At that time develop a plan and timetable to accomplish those goals.

Short of Acts of God like Hurricane Sandy or Katrina, when issues do arise, save the alibis as to why something didn't occur. Oversleeping, flat tires, running out of gas, babysitter was late aren't professional and sound even less professional when delivered as a reason for not meeting a business expectation. If you messed up, be human enough to admit it. I don't know about you, but I'm tired of hearing people blame McDonald's because they're overweight or blame the tobacco companies because they need oxygen to breathe.

Take ownership of your actions and you might be surprised at how much better a person you will become by being results driven.

Step 4 – If you haven't facilitated this by now, and I would strongly suggest this would be part of the sales process, schedule and conduct a tour of your facilities. This is especially important for distribution and manufacturing organizations. Use your facilities as a sales tool. This is a great time to discuss competitive differences with your various internal processes. This is where knowing your competitor plays a huge role. You don't need to mention your competitor by name or at all, just mention why the order picking system is a benefit to your client and what it means in terms of error- reduction, which in turn satisfies accurate line fill ratios, which eliminates returns and reorders. As mentioned before, when conducting a facilities tour, don't make the mistake of identifying various departments in the building. Translate the primary purpose the departments serve to the customer. If possible, have a respective department head give a brief summary of their department and how they support your particular customer. Make sure the facilities tour is not just a day out of the office for your client. They should go back to their office with a better understanding and comfort level of why they are working with you and your organization.

Step 5 – If permitted, schedule some social time with your buyer. This could be a lunch, dinner, ball game, concert, etc. However, before you go through with this, always check to make sure you are not violating any of your customer's company policies. More and more companies are regulating the vendor / buyer relationship. Don't do anything to jeopardize your hard work or the buyer's job.

Let's assume you are able to entertain our client. The first thing you want to know is their preferences; lunch or dinner – steak, fish, vegetarian, Vegan, Italian, Greek, Chinese, etc. Remember this is all about developing the relationship; it's not about your personal preferences. Back in my role of purchasing, I had a vendor who took me to the same restaurant every time we would go to lunch. I always appreciated the gesture, but the only thing on the menu that was palatable was the club sandwich. It wasn't a deal breaker, but a little variety would have been nice. This is a great segue into the next chapter – Selling Ethics.

Chapter 15

Selling Ethics

As stated in the previous chapter, know your customer's company's policies related to vendor gifts or gratuities. Some organizations spell everything out to the letter of the law of which every sentence begins with "no." Other companies leave it to the buyer's good judgment as to know right from wrong. I would strongly suggest that you review the policy with your customer. By doing this, you are protecting yourself and letting the buyer know that you are aware of the policy. That's not to say your buyer will not approach you for tickets for a ball game or play. At that stage you need to weigh the value of the account, your relationship with the buyer, and the risk involved if you are in violation of the company policy. My experience is that most companies have some sort of written policy, while at the same time it is loosely enforced. It would only come to light if there were obvious lack of services or product quality delivered versus written specifications. A good example of this would be a story that appeared in the local papers a few years ago. A building which was less than twenty years old was experiencing some challenges with the performance of concrete used is the construction. As it turned out, the concrete thickness was less then specified. As a result, areas of the building required renovation while at the same time displacing some tenants. This problem identified and exposed illegal activities from the contractor, building inspector, and a few others who were part of the skimming process.

A good buyer knows if their actions are in violation of their company's policy. I believe everyone has a moral compass and knows right from wrong in their hearts. I've had vendors approach me and offer the typical lunch or dinner. If we were, or if I was sure we would be doing business in the future, I didn't have a problem with the offer. If I viewed the offer as a way of "buying" my business, I would decline. The key is to know your buyer. Let the relationship develop on a professional level between both of you and your organizations. Don't ever give the impression that you are trying to buy their business. Earn and continue to earn their business and the gift issue will resolve itself. You will typically find organizations that implement stringent rules have had issues in the past and are just trying to protect themselves.

At one point I was working for an international organization that was setting up business in the Chicago area. The previous administrator had moved on and I assumed that role. It was a steady parade of vendors marching in and out of my office. The organization required a special format for a purchase order. I checked with the existing source my predecessor used and that turned out to be a disaster. Along with meeting him for the first time, I was told all that we were doing wrong with this form – not a good start. I then called on a former colleague who worked with specialty printers in the past. He referred me to a company that was more than willing to address my needs without the drama of the previous vendor. Met with the sales rep the next day and by the end of the week, I had my first proof that required a couple of minor corrections. Before the first vendor ever responded, I had the forms delivered. When the new printer delivered the first proof, he invited me to lunch. It was nothing fancy, just a nearby Italian restaurant that allowed us to further review our needs and their organization. I left that meeting feeling confident that this would be a very reliable printing source that would provide quality work. I'll cite one more example of questionable vendor judgment. In the aforementioned parade of vendors, the existing office supply vendor stopped in unannounced for a visit. I remember suggesting he schedule an appointment so we could spend some time reviewing the program. He eventually got the message when it became clear he didn't have my undivided attention. After our scheduled meeting, I received a Christmas gift of a $50 gift certificate and a nice designer travel bag. Ironically, during our meeting, I did inform him that I probably would be going out to bid in the next few months as I had intended to consolidate vendors and reduce our costs. I viewed the gifts as the supplier trying to buy my business. He didn't impress me as a trustworthy person to begin with and this just reinforced my suspicions. I promptly re-packaged the gifts and returned them with a note of appreciation, but I couldn't accept them. Ironically, when I did go out to bid, he called my assistant to see if she would get me copies of the bid responses. He promised her a new state-of-the-art vacuum cleaner. My assistant's response was hysterical. She told him she would check with me to see if it was okay if she did that. She told me he was so flustered, he begged her not to mention his idea to me. Needless to say, he never received another dime of my company's business. Another irony in all of this was about twenty years later, one of his former assistants worked for me at another organization. Somehow we got to talking about former employers and his name came up. I relayed my story about him and she laughed and said that was his way of doing business. By that time, he was out of business.

The previous examples relate to the obvious ethical issues in the business world. As the world has become smaller, we are facing new ethical standards related to gender and cultural differences. In the past thirty years, women have become a strong presence in the US work force. From successful entrepreneurs to CEO's, women have become a measurable force in the corporate America. As a result, attitudes and labor laws were also required to change. Comments such as "sweetie, dear, or honey," are no longer acceptable in the work place and have not been for quite some time. Continued use of those terms could result in a sexual harassment lawsuit.

My entre into the business world was working for a large international food manufacturer. In those days business attire at a minimum was a shirt, tie, and dress slacks for a man and a skirt and blouse or a dress for women. I can still remember the reaction to the memo from HR that stated women were now allowed to wear pant suits, which was revolutionary for that time. It was as though every woman received a pay raise. Looking back, it's almost comical to think that change had such a grand reaction.

Let's fast forward to the twenty first century. The business world has become one large melting pot of nationalities and cultures. Quite a few factors had an influence on these changes; corporate mergers, corporate expansion or relocation, open trade agreements, and the Internet. Navigating through the business world today has exposed us to a multitude of cultural differences and prejudices.

Much like any sales rep needs to know their audience prior to the presentation; the same philosophy applies today to your general work habits within your company or customer's facility. The statement, "everyone is entitled to their opinion," will always hold true; however, it's where and how you express that opinion that can amount to an ethical faux pas.

In my purchasing day, I had vendors make off-handed comments regarding minorities, thinking they were injecting humor in the conversation. My organization had an employee base comprised of 55% minorities, one of which was my secretary. Not that it was ever acceptable, but these vendors took a huge risk with their poor attempt at humor. While humor can certainly lighten up a moment and can be an asset in developing a relationship; poor attempts at humor can be devastating to a relationship or career as well.

In this multi-cultural world, the best action to take is to think about what you are going to say and the impact it will have on the people around you. If you have to think about it more than once, you probably should not say it. Most organizations now have policies governing harassment, which includes insensitive remarks, gestures, and actions. To successfully maneuver in today's world, know your audience and what is considered acceptable.

As I've stated before, you've worked so hard to develop the business relationship, don't destroy it because of an ignorant moment.

Chapter 16

Conclusion

From the beginning of time there were sales people in this world. The human who invented fire or the wheel had to have some way of selling his idea to other humans as a way of creating heat or improving mobility. A sale doesn't need to be performed in a suit with a PowerPoint presentation. Go to any super market or toy store in any country any day of the week and I promise you will see a child trying to sell his parent or guardian on buying them a toy or piece of candy. That is sales in its simplest form, but it is still sales.

The sales process is comparable to any sporting event. Golfers hit one shot to set up the next, baseball managers strategize on manufacturing runs, and football players are always trying to outsmart the person on the other side of the line. Winning at any of these sports, as well as sales, requires a well-developed strategy.

For the new sales rep, your key to success will center on developing the correct sales behaviors to employ on a consistent basis. From the beginning, these methods may seem like forced behavior as it may not be something that comes natural to you. At some point, you will incorporate these methods into your everyday behavior and way of selling and unconsciously employ them as part of the sales process.

I shared with you some of the viewpoints from the other side of the desk from my days in purchasing. These viewpoints should provide an insight as to how and what buyers perceive and the importance of delivering a clear and concise message. Never assume the buyer totally comprehends everything you are saying.

Remember, only you can develop your skills. You are in the driver's seat to achieve success.

As you read this book I hope you were able to develop additional concepts on how to improve your sales approach. Obviously every sales situation is different and no two customers are alike, but following the basic approaches outlined in the previous pages will help you get from concept to close in a successful manner.

Good Selling!

www.ingramcontent.com/pod-product-compliance
Lightning Source LLC
Chambersburg PA
CBHW071801200526
45167CB00017B/754